16 WEEKS TO A *FASTER* MARATHON

A Step-By-Step Guide that provides the specific workouts and knowledge you need to run your best Marathon yet

Brought to you by

RUNNERSCONNECT

TABLE OF CONTENTS

- Alternating tempos
- Tempo intervals
- How to recover from hard workouts
- Scheduling down weeks
- What to do when a workout doesn't go well

Part III: Marathon nutrition

- Preventing the "bonk"
- Developing and practicing your nutrition strategy
- Drinking and eating during the race
- Post-workout nutrition
- What to eat before a run
- Long runs on an empty stomach or fully fueled
- How to use energy gels
- Why you might not lose weight when marathon training
- Hydration
- Side stitches and cramps

Part IV: The marathon taper

- Common tapering mistakes
- Visualization to improve chances of success
- How to taper
- The last few days before the race
- 5-day pre-race nutrition plan
- Preparing for the elements

- The optimal marathon race plan

Part V: Sample training plan

- Sample intermediate training plan

Jeff Gaudette
Owner/CEO

Blake Boldon
Head Coach

Nate Jenkins
Assistant Coach

Casey Collins
Assistant Coach

Melanie Schorr, MD
Team Physician

Introduction

First, we want to say thank you for downloading the Ultimate Marathon Training Guide. This guide has been a labor of love and a collection of research, personal experience and conversations with some of the best coaches and minds in our sport. If you follow the principles outlined in this book, we are confident you can reinvigorate your marathon training, specifically target your body for success on race day and achieve the results you're looking for.

One of our main reasons for writing this guide was to provide a simple and practical handbook you can follow and implement into your own training plan. We've avoided a lot of the complicated physiological processes and theories involved in optimal marathon training so the guide would be as simple and easy to follow as we could possibly make it. If you have any questions, read anything you want to discuss in more detail or would like RunnersConnect to write you a custom training program, please don't hesitate to e-mail jeff@runnersconnect.net.

Finally, we want this information to benefit as many runners as possible. So, please feel free to e-mail it to all your running friends, share it via Facebook and Twitter, and get the word out. For my latest updates and information, you can visit our website, http://runnersconnect.net; follow us on Twitter @runners_connect; or join us on Facebook .

Happy Running,

The RunnersConnect Team

Part I

Marathon training concepts

Aerobic vs. anaerobic training

" The marathon is primarily an aerobic event as 99% of your energy contribution comes from aerobic respiration."

At the heart of all marathon training is the aerobic and anaerobic process. No matter your goals or ability level, the scientific fact is that, to run, your body needs to break down sugar and convert it to glycogen so it can be used as energy or fuel. When the body has an adequate supply of oxygen for this process, we call it aerobic respiration. When there is not enough oxygen, like when you are running hard at the end of a 5k, this is called anaerobic respiration.

Aerobic Running

Aerobic running or respiration occurs when your body has sufficient oxygen – like when you run easy miles with you friends. You breathe in, the body efficiently uses all the oxygen it needs to power the muscles, and you exhale. The waste products of aerobic respiration are carbon dioxide and water. These byproducts are easily expelled through the simple act of breathing. This is why your breath is carbon dioxide-rich and moist. Basically, when you are "running aerobically," your muscles have enough oxygen to produce all the energy they need to perform.

Anaerobic Running

Anaerobic respiration happens when there is NOT sufficient oxygen present. In this instance, the muscles do not have enough oxygen to create the energy you are demanding from them (like in an all-out sprint at the finish). When this happens, the muscles begin to break down sugar, but instead of producing CO_2 and water, your muscles produce lactic acid (that burning feeling in your muscles at the end of a race). Unfortunately, lactic acid is harder to remove than water and CO_2. Thus, lactic acid accumulates in your system, causing extreme fatigue.

The importance of understanding these definitions is clear. If you begin to run too hard in the middle of a workout or at the start of a race, your body goes into an anaerobic state, producing lactic acid. If you "go anaerobic" early in a race, you will feel fatigued sooner and become increasingly tired as the race progresses. Basically, the accumulation of lactic acid pools in your muscles and you have to slow down dramatically to get back to an aerobic state. If you go anaerobic too early, your chance at a personal record is out the window before the race is halfway over.

More importantly, in the marathon, running aerobically burns significantly less energy – and a greater percentage of fat compared with carbohydrates – than running anaerobically or below your aerobic threshold. Therefore, it is critical for the marathon that you learn to run aerobically and train your body to run faster while remaining above your aerobic threshold. To accomplish this, you want to perform tempo or threshold runs.

What is a tempo run?

In layman's terms, the production of lactic acid (the waste product of energy utilization) will remain relatively constant while running at an aerobic pace. At this aerobic pace, your body recycles lactic acid back into an energy source and efficiently expels the waste products. As you continue to run faster, the production of lactic acid will slowly increase. At some point (usually a specific pace per mile known as your lactate threshold), the production of lactic acid will soar and your body will no longer be able to convert it back into energy and expel the waste products. The lactic acid then floods into your muscles and causes that heavy, tired and burning feeling. Ultimately, lactic acid is one of the largest contributors to why you slow down as the race goes on.

In short, your threshold is defined as the fastest pace you can run without generating more lactic acid than your body can utilize and reconvert back into energy. This pace usually corresponds to a 10-mile or half-marathon race pace. Therefore, a tempo run or threshold run is basically a workout that is designed to have you running at just below or at your threshold pace.

But why is this important? By running just under your lactate threshold you can begin to decrease (or improve, depending on how you look at it) the pace at which you begin to produce too much lactic acid. For example, at the beginning of a training plan, your threshold might be 10 minutes per mile, which would mean you could run a half-marathon at this pace. As you do more tempo runs, your body gets stronger, adapts to the increased production of lactic acid and decreases this threshold pace to 9:30 per mile. Now, since your threshold is lower, you are able to run faster with less effort, which for the marathon means you can burn fuel more efficiently – saving it for the crucial last 10k.

What is a VO2max workout?

Defined simply, VO2max is the maximum amount of oxygen your body can utilize during exercise. Your VO2max is the single best measure of running fitness. Unfortunately (or fortunately, depending on how much you like lung-busting interval workouts), VO2max is not a big component of marathon training, but it is still useful, and it is important to include some VO2max workouts and speed work in your training plan.

Training at VO2max increases the amount of oxygen your body can use. Obviously, the more oxygen you can use, the faster you can run – that's a simple one. In addition, VO2max running can increase the efficiency of your running and improve your form. Since these workouts are faster, they force you to run more efficiently and with better form so you're able to hit the prescribed training paces.

Finally, training at VO2max also increases leg muscle strength and power, which improves economy (how much energy it takes to run at a certain speed). When muscles become stronger, fewer muscle cells need to contract to hit a particular pace; thus, the energy expenditure is lower, which can improve your fuel burning efficiency during a marathon.

How to breathe when running

Surprisingly, you're not alone if you've ever asked yourself how to breathe when running or solicited advice on breathing from your running partners. It's important for beginners to understand how they should approach the sport from the very basics.

Some people advocate breathing in through the mouth and out through the nose using slow breathing rhythms, and all sorts of similar nonsense. Nothing is as frustrating as the spread of misinformation, especially when it pertains to training topics. Therefore, let RunnersConnect help set the record straight.

Breathe through your nose or your mouth?

You should always breathe in and out primarily through your mouth. If your nose wants to join the party and help get air in and out, that's great. However, when you're running, feeding your muscles the oxygen they need is of paramount importance, and breathing through the mouth is the most effective way to inhale and exhale oxygen.

Breathing rhythm

Your exact breathing rhythm will depend on how hard or easy you are running and/or the intended intensity of your workout. Breathing rhythms refer to the number of steps you take with each foot while breathing in and out. For example, a 2:2 rhythm would mean you take two steps (one with your right foot and one with the left) while breathing in and two steps (again, one with your right foot and one with your left) while breathing out.

Easy runs

Typically, you'll find that a 3:3 rhythm (three steps – one with your left, one with your right, one with your left – while breathing in and three more – one with your right, one with your left, one with your right – while breathing out) works best for warm-ups and most easy-paced days. This allows plenty of oxygen to be inhaled through the lungs, processed and then exhaled with relative ease.

Don't try to force yourself into a 3:3 breathing rhythm on an easy day if it isn't feeling comfortable. Remember, the purpose of an easy day is to keep your effort comfortable and to help the body recover. If a 2:2 rhythm is more comfortable, go with it.

Breathing slower than a 3:3 rhythm is not advisable because you're not giving your body enough time to clear carbon dioxide. The average runner takes about 180 steps per minute (some a little less, others a little more), which means you take 90 steps with each foot in a one-minute span. A 3:3 rhythm enables you to take about 30 breaths per minute, ample time to process carbon dioxide while still getting in the oxygen you need.

Moderate-paced runs

Runs harder than an easy run, but not all-out race efforts, should typically be performed at a 2:2 ratio (two steps – one with your left, one with your right – while breathing in, two steps – one with your left, one with your right – while breathing out). A 2:2 breathing rhythm enables you take about 45 breaths per minute, which is perfect for steady state, tempo runs and marathon-pace runs.

Hard workouts and races

At the end of races or the end of a particularly hard interval session, 2:2 breathing might not cut it. In this case, you can switch to a 1:2 (one step breathing in, two steps breathing out) or 2:1 (two steps breathing in and one step breathing out) breathing rhythm. This will increase your oxygen uptake to 60 breaths per minute.

Avoid a 1:1 breathing pattern. At this rate, you'll be taking shallow breaths and you won't be able to inhale enough oxygen to maintain proper ventilation in the lungs.

You may not need to pay much attention to breathing rhythms at the end of races. Some runners prefer to run all out, focus on competing and let their breathing take care of itself. However, remembering breathing rhythms can be helpful to those runners who become anxious as the final meters approach.

Other good uses for breathing rhythms

While breathing rhythms can help you identify and monitor the intensity of your run, you can also use them to monitor and control other aspects of your training and racing.

Pacing

Paying close attention to your breathing rhythm can help you monitor and "feel" your pace, especially on tempo runs or tempo intervals. Once you lock onto your correct goal pace for the workout, you can monitor whether you begin to breathe faster or slower to identify when you accidentally speed up or slow down. It requires close attention to detail, but it can help for runners who struggle maintaining a consistent pace.

Hills

Many runners wonder how to adjust their pace when taking on a hill during a race. Unless you know the exact grade and length of a hill, it's very difficult to accurately measure how much you need to adjust your pace. However, if you're maintaining a 2:2 breathing rhythm through the race, then you should focus on maintaining that 2:2 rhythm as you tackle and crest the hill. By maintaining the same breathing rhythm, you keep your effort even and prevent yourself from spending too much energy getting over the hill.

As you can see, you have many ways that you can breathe and use rhythms to monitor your effort in workouts and races. Try not to become too focused on your exact breathing rhythm every step you take. Do what feels comfortable and you'll usually wind up falling into the proper rhythm by default.

Optimal stride rate

For both beginners and advanced runners, how to improve running form and technique is one of the most frequently asked questions. Unfortunately, it's also one of the most complex and variable components of training, both to adequately explain and for the runner to implement. Foot strike, turnover, paw back, knee lift: these are just a few of the terms used to describe the multitude of muscle movements, both conscious and subconscious, that go into every step you take. Isolating and improving these processes is difficult and can often distract a runner from the ultimate goal – running faster, running longer and staying injury-free.

Luckily, to get started on improving your running form, you can implement one simple trick that will help you develop a foundation for optimal running form and provide a building block for future improvements. So, what's this "secret" building block? Improving your stride rate.

What is stride rate?

Your stride rate is the number of steps you take per minute. Stride rate could also be called your running cadence or turnover. Calculating your stride rate is easy: simply count how many times your right foot hits the ground while running for one minute, and then multiply by 2. This number is your stride rate.

Why is stride rate important?

Improves your form

As previously mentioned, your stride rate is a fundamental building block to establishing good form. By implementing the proper turnover rate, you increase your chances of striking the ground at the correct angle and moving through the proper range of motion when your leg moves back, up and forward.

Improves your running economy

Running economy is a measure of how efficiently you use energy when running. It's exactly like the way a car measures miles per gallon. The more efficiently you run, the longer you can go before getting tired and the less effort you will use to run fast. Running with the optimal stride length maximizes your force on toe off (when your foot pushes you off the ground to move forward) and minimizes the time you spend in the air by controlling your stride length. These elements contribute to improving your efficiency.

Reduces your chance of injury

One of the main causes of running injuries is shock absorption, or lack thereof. If your stride rate is too low, you will spend more time moving up in the air, moving up and down as opposed to forward, and consequently land on the ground with more force. With the proper stride rate, you take lighter, quicker steps and reduce your chance of injury.

So what is the optimal stride rate?

The optimal stride rate is 180 steps per minute. That is 90 steps per minute with each foot.

Your stride rate doesn't change when you run faster or slower. Your stride rate remains the same at most normal speeds (very slow jogs or all-out sprints are exceptions). To run faster or slower, you simply change your stride length (a function of how forcefully you push off each foot) to speed up or slow down.

In 1984, Jack Daniels conducted a study on the stride rates of Olympic-caliber athletes from 3,000 meters to the marathon. Daniels found that all elite long-distance runners, male and female, had a stride rate unbelievably close to the 180 mark. It didn't matter if they finished first or last, or ran the 5k or the marathon, their stride rates were almost all the same.

How to improve your stride rate

If you want to improve your stride rate, focus on developing a 180-steps-per-minute turnover during your easy runs. On easy days, you have less to think about than tempo workouts or speed days.

Visualize

Imagine you're running on a road made of eggshells and you don't want to break them. Picture yourself floating over the ground quickly, with light, purposeful steps. Focus on running over the ground, not into it.

Metronome

If you run with music or a smart phone, consider installing a metronome app that you can set to a 180 bpm range. Focus on taking one step for every click of the metronome. You'll quickly fall into a natural 180-stride-per-minute rhythm and can turn off the metronome.

Likewise, music can throw off your stride rate. Many runners tend to naturally move to the beat of the music. If you want to improve your form, consider running sans music or with a metronome app instead.

Counting

If you do most of your runs technology free, you can simply count the number of steps you take with your right foot. Count for a minute and see how close to 90 steps per minute you get. Speed up or slow down your stride rate accordingly, and you'll soon find yourself running in a natural rhythm.

"Try a metronome app for your phone or ipod if you're having trouble finding a good 180 beat per minute rhythm."

Of course, you don't need to be exactly 180. A slight deviation like 175 or 185 is OK, too, as long as it feels comfortable for you. Stay close to the 180 range and you'll be on your way to improved running form before you know it.

Why runners get hurt

Runners primarily get injured for two reasons:

(1) Structural imbalances, such as having one leg shorter than the other or experiencing a severe weakness in a certain muscle group;

(2) Progressing their training volume and running speeds at a pace that their body is not ready to handle. Or, as RunnersConnect's Coach Jay would technically define it, "metabolic fitness precedes structural readiness."

"Your aerobic abilities progress faster than your muscle and ligaments, so you'll often feel fine running faster even if your body isn't ready for it - until you get injured."

Running coaches deal with both of these injury realities and often have confronted both in their own running careers. However, this ebook will focus on proper training progression, since structural imbalances need to be addressed outside the training cycle, usually with the help of a good physical therapist, podiatrist or chiropractor.

Don't be intimidated by the scientific aspect of training progression. This issue of structure vs. metabolism simply means that a runner's aerobic and anaerobic fitness develops at a faster rate than his or her tendons, ligaments, muscles and bones. To put it as simply as possible, you can hammer out a long run or a tempo run at 8 minutes per mile (or whatever your pace is), but your hips aren't yet strong enough to handle the stress of the pace or volume and your IT band becomes inflamed.

This experience is very common for runners who get recurring shin splints when they first start running. Their aerobic fitness is allowing them to continue to increase the distance of their runs because they no longer feel "winded" at the end of each run; however, their shin muscles haven't adapted to the increased pounding caused by the longer distance, and they quickly become injured.

A runner has two ways to combat these types of injuries: (1) continually address the structural system during training; and (2) progress the volume and speed work at a level the body is capable of adapting to.

To address the structural system, runners should start with a running-specific core routine so they can identify any weak areas.

By strengthening the core and running-specific muscles, runners can "speed up" the progress of the structural system and begin adding in longer and faster workouts earlier in the training cycle.

Furthermore, beginner runners or those who are unable to run the volume they desire can perform running-specific strength exercises that improve their strength and flexibility while still providing an aerobic component. To accomplish this, runners can perform a "circuit training" workout.

While addressing the structural aspect is important, the most critical component is ensuring that your training plan follows a patient and planned progression while gradually introducing running at your desired goal race distance and race pace.

Jumping into speed work too quickly

Generic schedules often include a quick progression from easy running to full-blown speed workouts. The transition from mainly easy aerobic runs to any form of speed work needs to be buffered with introductory speed dynamics, such as strides, hill sprints, steady runs and short fartleks. This concept is especially true for beginner runners.

Furthermore, most long-time runners have heard of the training concept known as the "base building" period. Base building refers to a portion of the training cycle in which the runner focuses on increasing mileage and forgoes harder workouts.

However, the traditional base building cycle contributes to most running injuries. While slowly increasing training volume is a good thing, most runners exit the base building cycle and introduce speed work too quickly. They've gone numerous weeks, or even months, without doing any type of speed work and expect to jump back into race pace without any consequence.

To combat this, runners need to include strides, hill sprints and even short fartleks in their training at all times. This doesn't mean runners have to be laser-focused year-round, but simply adding in a few strides and hill sprints a few times per week will go a long way toward warding off injuries.

In addition, you have to make sure that you take your easy runs slowly and give your body a chance to recover from the stress you're inducing.

Race-specific running

It is vital to train to the specific demands of the race. So, if you want to run 10k in 40 minutes, you need to train your body to do two things: (1) handle a 6:25 per mile pace without breaking down; and (2) handle a 6:25 mile pace for 6.2 miles without breaking down.

So, you first need to get your body adjusted to running 6:25 per mile. The first workout might look like: 12 x 400 @ 1:35 w/90 sec rest. Later in the training segment, as your body adjusts to the workload, your workout might become: 8 x 800 @ 3:12 w/90 sec rest. Now, you're doing 5 miles of volume at race pace instead of 3, but because you've slowly introduced work at race pace to your body, your structure is able to handle the stress. Your final workout 10 days before the race might look like: 10 x 1000 @ 4:00 w/90 sec rest, hammer # 5 and 8.

By being patient and gradually introducing both race-pace work and specific volume at race pace, you can hit all your time goals while staying injury free.

Why running faster is not always better

"Running faster than prescribed not only increases your chance of getting injured, it defeats the purpose of the workout."

Breaking the speed limit in a car is illegal, and it should be illegal in running workouts, too. In a runner's mind faster is always better, and any run that is longer or harder than prescribed is considered an achievement. However, if you're following RunnersConnect's or your coach's training, running faster or longer than prescribed might actually be detrimental to your potential success at your goal race and your long-term progression.

Each workout, recovery run and rest day in our training plans has a specific purpose. To maximize the effectiveness of each run and to make the absolute most out of every mile, it's important that you adhere to pace guidelines.

Here's a quick rundown of common running workouts and why breaking the speed limit is a bad idea:

Why running faster during tempo runs is detrimental

When you push too far beyond your lactate threshold pace, you prevent your body from learning how to effectively clear lactic acid. Instead of becoming more efficient by handling a moderate and consistent amount of lactate, your body is flooded. It isn't able to benefit from a prolonged period of lactate clearance. By speeding up, you don't achieve the benefits of the workout and actually walk away from your tempo run less fit than you would have by staying on the prescribed pace.

Why running too fast during recovery runs is detrimental

Your body does not have an infinite ability to heal itself and requires proper rest in between hard bouts. If you run too hard on an easy day, you create more muscle tears than you're fixing, extending the amount of time you need to fully recover. This can cause you to run poorly on subsequent workouts because your muscles are still fatigued. Keeping your easy days truly easy will promote faster recovery, allowing you to be prepared for the next hard session and produce maximum results.

Why running too fast during speed workouts is detrimental

During VO2max workouts and speed work, you're asking your body to push its limits. When running near your top speed, the likelihood of injury is increased since muscles are being contracted to their max while under duress. Your training schedule will assign workouts that hit your VO2max to develop speed, but keep you from going over the red line. Keeping your speed workouts within the given pace range will reduce the risk of injury and allow you to string together consistent training.

Our training plans are an intricate puzzle that pieces together different types of workouts. It maximizes the available time to prepare you to have your best performance on race day. Running faster than prescribed paces may seem as if it's advancing your fitness, but you are actually limiting your progress and increasing the likelihood of getting injured. Before you step out the door on your next run, think to yourself, "What is the purpose of my run today?" This will ensure you stay on course and give you the confidence you need to execute a plan as it's prescribed, even if it means obeying the speed limit.

Focusing on the right metrics

"The pace of your easy runs is a useless number. Your easy run pace is not indicative of fitness. Turn off the watch on your easy days and just focus on running comfortably."

Analyzing metrics in the workplace is a familiar concept. Whether it is counting the visitors to a website, calculating the number of widgets sold or measuring levels of employee satisfaction, we all have metrics in our daily lives that help us prioritize and assess the progress of our work.

Running is no different.

Runners implement metrics such as the speed of their tempo runs, the length of their long runs and a variety of other quantitative measurements to help them evaluate their development and ensure that they are on target to reach their goals.

However, as many business analysts will tell you, it's far too easy to get caught up in focusing on the wrong metrics. If you sell purple widgets, having 1 million visitors to your website is a huge accomplishment. But, if none of those visitors buy your purple widgets, it's a useless number.

In the working world, we're well educated and often quite aware of the temptation and potential pitfalls of concentrating on the wrong metrics. Businesses fail and people lose their jobs when we focus on the wrong business metrics. Unfortunately, many runners are not aware that they are often too concerned with the wrong metrics in their training. The result is often frustration, stagnant race results and injuries.

Here are a couple of common metrics many runners put too much focus on, and how you can shift your mind-set should you fall victim to these pitfalls.

Focusing on the pace of your easy runs

Want to know the most common question from RunnersConnect members, both veteran and beginner? "If I feel good, can I start running my easy runs faster?" Sometimes, this question gets asked as many as eight times in one week.

The problem isn't eight people asking the same question. The issue is that these runners are unnecessarily focused on the speed of their easy runs and think that by running faster on their easy days they will improve more rapidly.

Unfortunately, focusing on improving the pace of your easy runs is a vanity metric that does not correlate with your progress and contributes little to your fitness.

Aerobic development is roughly the same whether you're running at 30 seconds or 2 minutes slower than marathon pace. For a 3:30 marathoner, this means that an 8:30 pace provides basically the same aerobic benefits as miles at a 9:30 or 10:00 pace. However, running faster than an 8:30 pace only increases the time it takes for you to recover while providing little additional benefit aerobically. So, running faster is actually detrimental.

Probably the best example of how little your easy run pace matters is the training of Kenyan runners. Catherine Ndereba, who has a 2:18:47 marathon PR, often runs her easy run days at a 7:00 – 7:30 pace, which is about 2 minutes slower than her marathon pace. By keeping the easy days slow, Kenyan runners like Catherine are able to perform notoriously difficult workouts and take their performances to another level on race day. The Kenyans understand that increasing the pace on their easy days is not the most beneficial way to improve.

Your takeaway – Running faster on your easy days is not important, and it is not necessarily a sign of increasing fitness. Focus instead on the purpose of easy runs – recovering from hard workouts and preparing the body for upcoming sessions. When you stop thinking about pace and start concentrating on recovering, you'll be able to relax more and enjoy your easy runs for what they are – recovery.

Workouts are not designed to be a measurement of fitness

"Workouts are not designed to measure your fitness or predict how well you will run at your goal race."

It's easy to get frustrated and feel like you're going backwards after a tough workout. Everyone has had more than a few training sessions that lead them to wonder if they had somehow completely lost it. After seeing one rough workout three weeks before an important 10k, one coach said something unforgettable: "Workouts are for improving specific physiological systems, not for proving how fit you are. You prove your fitness on race day." This statement should hit home with everyone.

When analyzing workouts, it's tempting to compare splits and workout times to potential race performances. However, the two rarely correlate.

Perhaps you're working on speed, which is a weakness for your predominantly slow-twitch muscles, or you're heading into the workout with tired legs to help simulate marathon fatigue. Regardless, you may find yourself running slower than expected or struggling to maintain race pace. This can be frustrating and demoralizing if you're always looking to measure your workout performance with race potential.

However, if you focus instead on executing the purpose of the workout and completing it to the best of your ability, you're making progress physiologically, which will ultimately lead to a personal best on race day.

Your takeaway – You should only use your workouts to measure progress when compared with similar workouts under similar conditions, not as a measurement of race times or potential. Remember, workouts are for improving specific physiological systems, not for proving how fit you are. You prove your fitness on race day.

The next time you're analyzing your training or looking for areas to improve, make sure you're evaluating the right metrics or you could find yourself working hard with nothing to show for it.

How long before you benefit from a workout

It's the question all runners want to know – "How long will it be before I see the benefits from my workout?" Unfortunately, like most aspects of running and training, there isn't a quick and easy answer.

Most experienced runners have heard that it takes 10 days to realize the benefits of a workout. While this is a good rule of thumb to follow, especially during the taper phase of a training plan, it's not a very accurate measurement of how your body responds and adapts to a myriad of different training factors. For example, the exact rate your body absorbs and responds to a workout is going to be influenced by the type of workout, the intensity, your recovery protocol and your body's own rate of adaptation.

However, while there is no universal and simple answer to this question, if we take the time to break down all the factors that affect workout absorption, you can extrapolate a fairly accurate estimation of how long it will take to benefit from each type of workout on your training schedule.

"Recovering from hard workouts is as, if not more, important than the actual workout itself."

Like any analysis that involves a myriad of influencing factors, the first thing to do is establish assumptions and control some of the influencing variables.

First, for the purpose of this in-depth breakdown, assume that you're implementing a thorough recovery plan, doing three things after each workout: (1) fueling properly; (2) getting plenty of sleep; and (3) stretching or massaging to reduce soreness. Certainly, you can be doing more to speed your recovery, but this is the baseline for general workout adaptations.

Second, make an assumption about your general rate of recovery. It's unfortunate, but some runners have the ability to recover faster than their peers. Everyone has that running pal who seems to bounce back from track workouts like she didn't even run the day before (if you don't know someone like this, then you're the envy of all your running friends because you're "that guy"). Likewise, runners generally recover slower as they get older. Typically, a 65-year-old is going to take longer to recover from a hard workout than a spry runner in his mid-20s. For the sake of keeping things simple, assume your rate of recovery is about average for a 35- to 40-year-old runner. If you're older or have found that you recover much faster than your running peers, you'll be closer to the outer numbers of the ranges presented below.

How long it will take to benefit from each type of workout

As mentioned previously, the type of workout you perform and the intensity at which you run it will determine how quickly you see benefits. Why? Because your cardio-respiratory, muscular and nervous systems all respond to training at a different rate. Since each type of workout is designed to stress a particular physiological system, the rate of adaptation will vary.

To make it simple, here is how quickly you'll reap the benefits from each type of workout on your training schedule:

Speed development

Speed development workouts target the nervous system and are designed to develop the communication between your brain and your muscles. More importantly, improvements to the nervous system allow your brain to activate a greater percentage of muscle fibers and fire them more forcefully.

Speed development workouts aren't the type of speed work most runners think about. Instead of lung-busting intervals, you're doing short, full-speed repetitions on full recovery. Examples of speed development workouts include explosive hill sprints, in-and-out 150s, or 200m repeats with full recovery – the type of stuff you see sprinters do on the track.

Luckily, **you can reap the benefits from a speed workout very quickly – within a day or two**. The nervous system responds quickly to new stimuli because the growth and recovery cycle is very short – according to this study, it's the same principle behind an extensive warm-up that involves dynamic stretching and strides. The nervous system responds very quickly to new stimuli and changes.

VO2max and hill work

VO2max and hill workouts are designed to develop your anaerobic capacity, or your ability to withstand a large amount of oxygen debt, and your muscular system.

Unfortunately, muscle strength and anaerobic capacity take longer to develop because of the intense demand on the body and the amount of time it takes for the muscle fibers to recover after intense sessions. Therefore, **it**

takes anywhere from 10-14 days to realize the full benefit from an anaerobic capacity workout.

You should also note that because of the demanding nature of these workouts, you may actually feel like you've "lost fitness" for 7-8 days after these workouts. We all know running the day after an intense session of 400s can be difficult, but the performance loss will carry through for a few extra days, so be wary.

Threshold runs

Threshold runs, tempo runs and marathon pace runs are designed to train your body to increase its ability to reconvert lactate back into energy. In general, these types of workouts are taxing, but they aren't slugfests like a VO2max workout might be. Therefore, the recovery cycle after a tempo run is faster, which enables you **to reap the benefits from the workout within 7-10 days.**

Long runs

Finally, the goal of a long run is to build up your aerobic system. Primarily, this is accomplished by increasing the number and size of the mitochondria in your muscle fibers, increasing the number of capillaries and increasing the myoglobin content of your muscle fibers.

While these improvements to the aerobic system are great for long-term development, you don't often "feel" the benefit from them right away. It can take four to six weeks to notice changes in your aerobic ability and for the actual training effect being felt. Likewise, the more experienced you are, the less you will "feel" the benefits from a long run, since your aerobic system is already quite developed.

Here's a quick and easy chart that breaks down the general timeframe it takes to realize the benefits from each particular workout:

Workout type	Intensity/difficulty	When you'll see benefits
Speed development	Hard	1-3 days
	Medium	1-3 days
VO2max/Hills	Hard	12-15 days
	Medium	9-11 days
Threshold	Hard	10-12 days
	Medium	7-10 days
Long Run	Hard or Medium	4-6 weeks

This chart makes it easy to see why a general 10-day rule is applied, but isn't always an accurate assessment of when you'll realize the benefits from a session.

Treadmill vs. running outside

Is running on a treadmill the same as running outside? It's a common question and, despite conflicting opinions, scientific research has shown that running on the treadmill has roughly the same effect as running outside if you make a few simple adjustments. In fact, there are some types of workouts you can do better on a treadmill than you can do outside. However, running on a treadmill does have its disadvantages and, for some runners, a mile on the "hamster wheel" feels like 10 miles outdoors.

So, in this section, you will learn the potential positives and negatives of treadmill running, how to adjust your workouts to make treadmill running equivalent to logging miles outdoors, and some tips to make treadmill running more "enjoyable" when it's necessary.

The first thing we need to examine is whether running on a treadmill is the same as running outside.

On one hand, with a treadmill, the belt is moving under you and there is no wind resistance for your body to counter, so it should be easier to run. Theoretically, you could jump up and down on a treadmill and it would record that you're running at whatever speed the belt is moving. Outside, your legs have to propel your motion forward while pushing through the resulting wind resistance (however minor it may be).

Luckily, scientific research has proven that **setting the treadmill to a 1% grade accurately reflects the energy costs and simulates outdoor running**. Therefore, by setting the treadmill to a 1% grade, you can offset the lack of wind resistance and the belt moving under you to make treadmill running the same effort as running outdoors.

Corroborating research has shown that VO2max is the same when running on a treadmill compared to outside, clearly demonstrating that running on a treadmill is as effective as running outside. Furthermore, research reveals that bio-mechanical patterns did not change when test subjects ran on a treadmill vs. when they ran outside.

Therefore, we can decisively conclude that **running on a treadmill has the same effect as running outside when the treadmill is at a 1% grade.**

Benefits of treadmill running vs. outdoor running

Because we now know that running outside and running on the treadmill are basically the same at a 1% grade, we can identify the specific workouts or instances when running on a treadmill might actually be better than running outside.

When the weather and footing are bad

This is the most obvious benefit of treadmill running, but it's important to include because elements affect every runner differently. Some people have a very difficult time when it's hot or there is bad footing; however, put them on a clear road on a cold or rainy day and they are machines. You may be the opposite, so don't be afraid to hit the treadmill on the days you need to. Getting in a good workout on the treadmill is better than suffering through a bad run or getting hurt.

Simulating race courses while indoors

One of the distinct benefits of a treadmill is the ability to simulate your goal race course. Many of the more advanced treadmills allow you create your own unique course profile, which you can use to simulate the exact course you're training for. Just program the machine or, if you don't have that option, manually adjust the incline levels based on the course map, and you can train on the course any day of the week.

For runners training for the Boston marathon, you can even put lifts under the back end of the treadmill to simulate downhill running. You can now simulate the pounding of the downhills on your quads and be better prepared for the opening miles on race day.

Fluid and carbohydrate intake

It's critical that you practice taking in fluids and carbohydrates on your runs to teach yourself how to eat and drink without stopping. Obviously, this can be a logistical nightmare if you don't plan on carrying your water or gels with you. Running a tempo run or long run on the treadmill will allow you to practice eating and drinking without slowing down. While the treadmill won't make the actual act of eating or drinking any easier, it can make it logistically possible.

Disadvantages of treadmill running vs. outdoor running

While running on the treadmill can have some distinct advantages, it can also be detrimental to your long-term development if the only time you run outside is to race. Here are some specific areas you need to watch out for if you're a habitual treadmill runner:

You don't learn how to pace on a treadmill

When running on a treadmill, it's easy to "set it and forget it" and just lock into a target pace. Unfortunately, this method doesn't teach you how to properly find and maintain pace on your own. As a consequence, you stunt the development of your internal effort and pacing instincts. On race day, when executing race splits is critical, you won't have developed that fine sense of pacing that is crucial to running a negative split and finishing strong.

The treadmill is boring

For the majority of runners, running on the treadmill is boring. Without scenery passing you by and something to take your mind off the blinking lights in front of you, it's too easy to look at the clock every 30 seconds and get discouraged that more time hasn't passed since your last glance. Likewise, when you're running a tough workout outside, you can "feel" the finish line getting closer and you have a more natural sense of the distance remaining. On a treadmill, your mind can't visualize the finish line, so it becomes harder to concentrate when the pace gets hard and you need to push yourself.

Generally, you should approach running on a treadmill like you should with everything in life – in moderation. The treadmill can be a great training tool and essential for those runners who live in harsh weather environments (both hot and cold). However, don't neglect the specific skills you need to develop by running outside on occasion.

How to run hills

Whether you encounter hills in training or on the race course, fighting gravity can quickly become an epic struggle both mentally and physically. However, running hills doesn't have to ruin your workout or race. By maintaining proper form and executing a smart strategy as you run up and over them, you can actually turn hill running into a strength you can capitalize on.

In this section, you will learn some simple form tweaks that can save you energy and help you breeze up and over hills with greater ease. Likewise, RunnersConnect will share its secret to attacking hills during a race so you can maintain pace and stay on track to reach your goal time.

Running form on hills

Running uphill and downhill require some slight tweaks to your form to maximize your power and efficiency as well as provide you much-needed oxygen. Many magazines and training partners will give you pointers on proper form, but it's important you are able to properly visualize the tips, or you could end up doing more harm than good. Here are our form suggestions and a visual for how to implement them.

Running uphill

(1) The most critical element is that you keep your chest up and open. The most common advice you might have received is to "lean into the hill." Unfortunately, this causes many runners to hunch at the waist to lean forward.

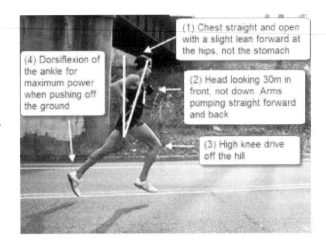

This constricts your airway and makes it harder to breathe deeply. You do need to lean forward, but make sure you lean at the hips, not the waist.

(2) Keep your head and eyes up, looking about 30 meters in front of you. Dropping your head restricts how much oxygen you can take in and will cause you to slouch. Likewise, drive your arms straight forward and back and use them as pistons. Your arms should form a 90-degree angle at the elbow, and swing straight back and forth, not across your body.

(3) Focus on driving your knee off the hill, not into the hill like you might do if you maintained your normal knee drive. Work on landing on the ball of your foot to spring up the hill.

(4) Dorsiflex your foot at the ankle – dorsiflexion is when you point your toes towards the ground. Think of yourself exploding off your ankle and using that last bit of power to propel you up the hill with minimal energy expenditure. Focusing on dorsiflexion can save you a lot of energy and really help you get up the hill faster and with less energy.

Downhill running

(1) Just like when running uphill, you want to have a slight lean forward at the hips to take advantage of the downhill. Don't overdo the lean; you just need a slight tilt to benefit from gravity.

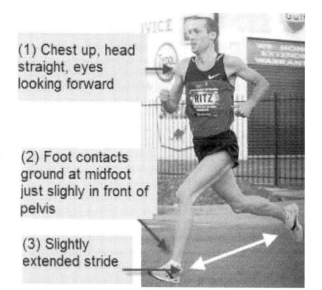

(1) Chest up, head straight, eyes looking forward

(2) Foot contacts ground at midfoot just slighly in front of pelvis

(3) Slightly extended stride

Keep your arms relaxed and only slightly moving forward and back. Don't flail them to the sides; this will waste energy. Likewise, keep your head up and your eyes looking forward.

(2) You want to land with your foot either right beneath your torso or just slightly in front of your pelvis, depending on the grade of the downhill (the steeper the grade, the more likely your foot is to land out in front). Extending your leg too much will cause you to land on your heel, which will act like a breaking motion. Focus on landing toward your midfoot to maintain speed while staying in control.

(3) Your stride length should naturally be extended when running downhill. However, you shouldn't need to consciously increase your stride length. The pace and the grade of the hill will do this naturally for you.

Pacing during hilly races

Tackling hills during races or even important workouts can be daunting. It's easy to ruin your race by wasting too much energy grinding up a hill or lose big chunks of time by slowing the pace too much. To handle hills effectively in races, learn to run up and down them by **effort**, not pace.

When you approach the base of a hill, you should already have a good feel for the effort you're maintaining to keep the pace you need. Meaning, if you're running goal race pace already, you should already know what that pace "feels" like. So, when you begin to ascend up the hill, **focus on maintaining the same effort**. Obviously, your actual pace will slow, even though you're running the same effort (don't worry, you'll make it up on the downhill). The exact time you'll "lose" on the uphill will be a function of the steepness and length of the hill.

Now, when you crest the hill and begin the descent, simply maintain the same effort that it took to run your goal pace before you started going up the hill. Contrary to running uphill, this effort will now make your actual pace faster than goal pace. For the most part, this will largely negate most of the time you lost going uphill, and you'll reach the bottom still on target.

The secret behind this strategy is that by maintaining a consistent effort, you won't lose crucial energy pushing either up or down the hill. Therefore, instead of becoming an energy-sapping obstacle, the hill will be just another bump in the road and you'll be able to maintain your pace and stay strong over the remainder of the course.

By improving your form and implementing this simple strategy, you'll be able to conquer hills of all lengths and inclines.

The myth of the 20-miler

The marathon long run is overrated... Pause until the sound of your gasp fades. RunnersConnect sees too many runners focus on trying to get in multiple 20- or 22-milers during their training segment, at the expense of improving more important physiological systems. More importantly, runs of over 3 hours offer little aerobic benefit and significantly increase injury risk.

Instead, your training should focus on improving your aerobic threshold, teaching your body to use fat as a fuel source and building your overall tolerance for running on tired legs through accumulated fatigue. Since the long run is such an ingrained element of marathon training, suggesting they are overrated almost sounds blasphemous. But take a look at some scientific research, relevant examples and suggestions on how to better structure your training to support this claim and help you run your next marathon faster.

The science

Most runners training for a marathon are averaging anywhere from 9 minutes to 12 minutes per mile on their long runs (3:45 to 5-hour finishing time). At a pace of 10 minutes per mile, a runner will take roughly 3:30 to finish a 21-mile run. While there is no doubt that a 21-mile run (or longer) can be a great confidence booster, from a training and physiological standpoint, it doesn't make too much sense. Here's why:

Recent research has shown that your body doesn't see a significant increase in training benefits after running for 3 hours. The majority of physiological stimulus of long runs occurs between the 90-minute and 2:30 mark. This means that after running for 3 hours, aerobic benefits (capillary building, mitochondrial development) begin to actually stagnate or decline instead of getting better. So, a long run of over 3 hours builds about as much fitness as one lasting 2:30.

To add insult to injury, running for longer than 3 hours significantly increases your chance of injury. Your form begins to break down, your major muscles become weak and susceptible to injury and overuse injuries begin to take their toll. This risk is more prevalent for beginning runners whose aerobic capabilities (because of cross-training and other activities) exceed their musculoskeletal readiness. Basically, their bodies aren't ready to handle what their lungs can.

Not only are aerobic benefits diminished while injury risk rises, recovery time is significantly lengthened. The total amount of time on your feet during a 3-plus-hour run will break down the muscles and completely exhaust you, which leads to a significant delay in recovery time and means you can't complete more marathon-specific workouts throughout the following week, which research has shown are a more important component to marathon success.

Why is the long run so popular?

Given the overwhelming scientific evidence against long runs of over 3 hours, why are they so prevalent in marathon training?

First, many people have a mental hurdle when it comes to the 20-mile distance. The marathon is the only distance that you can't safely run in training before your goal race. Therefore, like the 4-minute mile and the 100-mile week, the 20-mile-long run becomes a mental barrier that feels like a reachable focus point. Once you can get that 2 in front of your total for the day, you should have no problem running the last 10k. Unfortunately, this just isn't true from a physiological standpoint.

Second, the foundation for marathon training still comes from the 1970s and 1980s, at the beginning of the running boom. Marathoning hadn't quite hit the numbers it has today (you could sign up for most marathons, including Boston, the day before the race) and the average finishing time at most races was 3 hours (today that number is near 4 hours).

Therefore, the basis for how to train for a marathon came from runners who averaged close to 6 minutes per mile for the entire race. So, 20- and 22-milers were common for these athletes, as a run of this distance would take them about 2:30 to finish at an easy pace.

Moreover, when you hear the term "hitting the wall" you immediately think of the 20-mile distance. "Hitting the wall" frequently occurred at 20 miles because your body can store, on average, 2 hours of glycogen when running at marathon pace. Two hours for a 6-minute mile marathoner occurs almost exactly at 20 miles.

In short, the basis for a lot of our notions and understanding of marathon training is passed down from generation to generation without regard for the current paces of today's marathoners. Therefore, we also need to reassess where the long run fits into the training cycle and how we can get the most benefit from training, week in and week out.

How to train better

RunnersConnect's training plans downplay the role of the long run and instead focus on improving your aerobic threshold (the fastest pace you can run aerobically and burn fat efficiently) and utilizes the theory of accumulated fatigue to get your legs prepared to handle the full 26 miles.

For example, our training plans string out the workouts and mileage over the course of the week, which increases the total amount of quality running you can do along with decreasing the potential for injury. We shorten your long run to the 16- to 18-mile range and buttress it against a shorter, but steadily paced run the day before. This will simulate the fatigue you'll experience at the end of the race, but reduce your risk of injury and excess fatigue. As a side note, we also implement this training philosophy for the half-marathon distance. By adding a steady run the day before the long run, you can simulate late-race fatigue without having to run the full distance, and teach your body how to finish strong and fast.

In addition, when you have shorter long runs, you're able to increase the total quality and quantity of tempo and aerobic threshold workouts throughout your training week. Instead of needing 4-5 days to fully recover from a 3-hour-plus run, **we can recover in one or two days and get in more total work at marathon pace or faster.** Developing your aerobic threshold is the most important training adaptation to get faster at the marathon distance because it lowers the effort level required to run goal pace and teaches your body how to conserve fuel while running at marathon pace.

Finally, with a focus on shorter, more frequent long runs, you can implement faster training elements, such as fast-finish long runs, which allow you to increase the overall quality of your long runs. These fast-finish long runs help you increase the pace of the overall run, get you familiar and adapted to running marathon pace while tired and also increase your body's ability to store energy for the end of the race and use fat as a fuel source more efficiently.

When you balance out the gains you can get from finishing a long run fast and upbeat with the negatives from an extended long run, you can see why a shorter, faster long run is the better training option for almost all marathoners aiming to finish slower than 3:30.

Part II

Marathon-specific workouts

How to warm up

The warm-up is an important part of any workout, and one of the most important aspects of a good race. A good warm-up helps prepare the body to **run hard, race fast**, and will help make your workouts easier and more productive.

Basically, the warm-up is designed to get the **blood flowing to your legs**, which makes them looser and ready for hard work. Warming up before a hard workout or race also helps **ward off injuries** by ensuring that muscles are warm and loose before any hard running begins. The following are the steps you should take to get in a good warm-up:

1. The warm-up should begin with easy running for the specified amount of time on your schedule. The pace doesn't matter, but it should feel slow and easy. You're not trying to set any records, just get the body primed for a good race or workout.

 2. After the run, stop and stretch for 5 to 10 minutes. Stretching when your muscles are warm helps increase its effectiveness. You should focus on any muscles that are sore and tight or run through a general routine to hit all the major muscle groups.

3. After some light stretching, run 2 x 30 sec strides at a little faster than your goal pace, with a full 2 or 3 minutes rest between the two. This is a crucial step that most people forget to do. The strides help send the signal to the body that **it's time to work hard** and get your **heart rate elevated**. This will help you get on pace the first interval or mile and make it feel easier, since the body won't be in shock. If you're racing a shorter race, you can also add

in two more 20-second strides at a faster pace to help get the "pop" in your legs.

After these simple steps, you'll be primed to run a great race or workout.

After the race or workout, give yourself a few minutes to catch your breath, say hi to friends if you're at a race, get some water and start feeling good again.

When you feel like you're recovered, run the specified number of miles on your schedule for your cool down. The pace should be very easy and at a pace slower than you may even run on your easy days. The pace doesn't matter. The focus of the cool down is on loosening up your tight muscles and gradually getting oxygen- and nutrient-rich blood to your legs.

Reward yourself with a recovery drink or snack and pat yourself on the back for a job well done!

Speaking of stretching

While no one would argue that a good diet and a reasonable training schedule are invaluable in preventing injuries, there's a surprising amount of controversy regarding the role of stretching.

Some people swear by it, while others shun it. Of those who do stretch, some emphasize stretching before working out, while others stretch only after exercise. Let's look at what research says about the role of stretching in preventing injuries.

In one of the largest studies conducted on the importance of stretching, Dr. Herbert Pope concluded that stretching before physical activity had no effect on injury frequency in athletes (Med Sci Sports Exercise, 2000; 32 (2): 271-277).

This finding is consistent with several other studies that have demonstrated that stretching, particularly stretching before activity, plays little to no role in injury prevention.

However, this study failed to include the effects of stretching after exercise. Luckily, in 2005, a group of Australian doctors set up a study to measure the effects of stretching after exercise and whether it reduced hamstring injuries. At the end of the study, the stretching program decreased hamstring injury rates from an average of 10 athletes per season to three athletes per season. Also, the number of days lost from competition was reduced from 35 days in the no-stretch group to 10 days in the stretching group.

Not only did this study show that stretching after exercise was beneficial, these findings are consistent with other studies that demonstrate that muscle tightness is a predictor of injury and that increasing flexibility by stretching reduces injury rates.

So now that we have proven that stretching after exercise does help prevent injuries, the question remains as to what type of stretching is best suited to accomplishing this result. Research has proven that stretching with mild to moderate force for 15 to 30 seconds two to three times is the most effective method to increase muscle length and reduce injury. There were no additional benefits to stretching to the point of pain, longer than 35 seconds or more than four times.

The lessons to be learned from these studies are clear:

1. Avoid pre-exercise stretching. That means no stretching when your muscles are not warmed up.

2. Never stretch to the point of discomfort. After your run, perform a few 15- to 30-second stretches on each of the major muscle groups. Never push the stretch to the point of discomfort. It's better to hold a stretch for 15 seconds and repeat it throughout the day than to spend long periods stretching specific muscles.

Threshold intervals

Now that this ebook has covered VO2max workouts and tempo runs and the relative importance of each during marathon training, how can you work on running faster (mechanics, speed, form and efficiency) while not deviating from the long-term goal of progressing aerobic fitness? Simple: you implement faster-paced intervals at 8k to 10k paces with a short amount of rest – what are called threshold intervals.

When designing running workouts, a coach can manipulate three elements of the training plan to elicit certain physiological adaptations. These three elements are: (1) the time or distance of the interval; (2) the speed or pace at which you need to run the workout; and (3) the amount of rest you can take between efforts. While many people are familiar with the ability to change the distance and pace of an interval – and how this can affect fitness – the rest portion of a workout is often an afterthought or the forgotten element in the training equation, especially for those writing their own schedules.

In actuality, manipulating the rest portion of a track workout is particularly effective and one of the best ways to gain fitness. As this ebook has mentioned, improving your aerobic threshold is one of the most effective ways to gain fitness and race faster at the marathon distance. By varying the rest during interval workouts in a distinctive and innovative way, you can get the benefits of both a tempo run and a speed workout.

These intervals allow you to run much faster than a tempo run (usually 6 to 7 percent faster), but because of the short rest, you can maintain a threshold effort. During these threshold intervals, you'll often barely catch your breath before starting the next interval, but that means the workout will also go by quickly.

The added bonus of performing these intervals is the pacing practice and strategies you can develop. If you start out too fast during the first interval or two, the short rest will come back to bite you during the middle and latter part of the workout. You may feel good going faster for the first three or four intervals, but the big hairy gorilla will jump on your back during the second half and make the rest of the workout a struggle and a test of wills. This will help you simulate the fatigue you'll experience in the marathon and teach you to control your pacing during the first half of the race.

When performing threshold intervals, it is important to pay attention to the paces and the rest. If you begin to feel tired during the workout and your paces start to slow, make sure you continue to maintain the timing of the rest. You can slow down if you need to, but keep the rest the same.

Steady runs

Steady runs, or steady-state runs as some literature refers to them, are a great way to build aerobic strength, which is the foundation for your best performances in the marathon. Simply speaking, steady runs are efforts that are about 20 to 30 seconds slower than marathon pace. You will find different definitions of a "steady run pace" on the Internet and from different coaches, but this definition is specific to marathon training.

As is the case with all running workouts, you should use steady runs to elicit a multitude of performance- and fitness-enhancing benefits. The exact benefits largely depend on the desired goal of the session and how they're implemented.

The reason for steady running

Steady runs accomplish three different types of objectives and training stimuli:

1. Starter workouts

Because steady runs should be about 20 or 30 seconds slower than marathon pace, they ease athletes into workouts when they are just starting the training schedule, as an introductory workout, or if they have not done structured workouts before. Twenty or 30 seconds slower than marathon pace will usually be "comfortably hard," which is perfect when the objective is to add a little bit of hard running to the schedule, but not go overboard.

2. Building aerobic strength

Building aerobic strength is one of the most important pieces of the training puzzle to make you faster at the marathon. The hard part is that developing aerobic strength takes time. Luckily, steady runs facilitate the development of aerobic strength by challenging your aerobic system, but not making you too tired to run hard the next day. Some more experienced and veteran marathon runners train using a medium-long steady run sometime during the middle of the week, which helps add a new stimulus and an opportunity for increased aerobic development.

3. Marathon training

Training for the marathon is different from training for shorter distances. Mainly, this is because you have to train specifically for two additional things

– running on tired legs and learning to burn fuel more efficiently. Steady runs help increase the total amount of quality miles (quality miles being miles run at or near marathon pace) an athlete can run during a marathon-training block. Mainly, steady runs should be run the day before a long run, adding a slight amount of fatigue to the legs, which better simulates the tired feeling at the end of a marathon without having to run 26 miles.

How to perform a steady run

Steady runs should be performed like mini-workouts. The pace should be comfortably hard (usually 20 to 30 seconds slower than marathon pace).

1. Start each steady run with a mile at normal easy pace. Keep the pace easy; this mile is a warm-up mile to get the blood flowing to the legs and loosen up your muscles.

2. After the first easy mile, take a brief minute or two to stretch anything that is tight, sore or that has been bothering you lately.

3. Ease into the steady pace over the next mile or two. You don't have to go from a standing start to steady pace in the first 100 meters. Let your body fall into the pace naturally. Some days this will feel easy and other days getting down to steady pace will be a challenge.

4. Because steady runs are usually a little longer than tempo runs, you'll have to work on concentrating over a longer distance. Work on staying focused throughout the run and concentrating on your pace and effort. This is great practice for race day.

5. Use the last mile as a mini-cool down. Bring the pace back down to an easy pace and enjoy the feeling of job well done. The cool down will help your muscles relax and start the recovery process.

Surges during your long run

The long run has the potential to be more than just time on your feet with long, slow miles. While fast-finish long runs are quickly becoming a fundamental element in advanced training programs, an underutilized and rarely mentioned workout involves surges during the long run.

Implementing planned surges during a long run serves a multitude of purposes. First, you can inject speed into a training plan during what would otherwise be a "slow" running day. Second, you can learn to run fast while fatigued, which develops race-specific strength and skills. Finally, surges help increase the overall quality and pace of your long run, thus enabling you to finish faster.

Speed in disguise

One trick is to "disguise" speed within training programs. It is essential to insert some sort of speed development into the training plan at least four or five days per week. Speed training helps improve running mechanics, increases efficiency and buffers the body for race pace or faster efforts.

However, speed development doesn't have to occur all in one workout. You can spread speed training throughout the week in small doses, which enables you to maximize your time spent developing the more important physiological elements, such as threshold and aerobic strength, while also reducing the risk of injury associated with speed work. By adding surges to a long run, you can go from zero minutes spent working on speed, mechanics and efficiency to 10 or even 15 minutes of "disguised" speed training per week. This slight increase in speed development is all you need to start seeing dramatic results in your mechanics and overall speed.

One of the most difficult aspects of racing is realizing that, as the race goes on, you have to keep working harder to maintain the same pace. Anyone who has ever raced at any distance knows that the first mile is significantly easier than the last mile. The increase in difficulty is caused by fatigue. Therefore, anything you can do in your training to improve your ability to run faster while tired is going to lead to better race results. By injecting surges into your long run, you develop the specific physiological adaptations and mental skills necessary to increase your effort and pace as the race gets more difficult.

In addition, when you're training for a marathon, surges late into a long run, especially when you're low on fuel, help teach your body to burn fat more efficiently at race pace. Why is this important? Typically, the faster you attempt to run, the greater percentage of carbohydrates you burn (since carbohydrates are converted to energy quickly). Therefore, if you can increase the percentage of fat burned for energy while at race pace, you'll have more carbohydrates to burn late in the race. You can read more about this in Part III of this book, "Marathon Nutrition."

Quality

When doing surges during the middle of the run, you will typically notice two things: (1) the first surge is always the hardest; and (2) once you slow back down to your normal long run pace, you will find your "easy" pace is now faster than before the surge.

The first surge is always the hardest because you have to wake your body up. As runners, we've been conditioned to think of long runs as slow and leisurely Sunday strolls. (Granted, running slow for your long runs is appropriate at times, especially after a hard week of workouts or following an increase in volume.) Therefore, the body and mind aren't ready for the hard interval you're about to throw in. Luckily, as your body and mind get adjusted to the speed, you'll start to feel invigorated by the change of pace. You will also notice the pace increase bleeds into the recovery portion of the workout and you will find yourself running a faster overall long run than you normally would without surges.

How to incorporate surges

Long run surges should begin about halfway through the intended long run distance and end about 75 to 80 percent of the way through the run. This means if you have a 10-mile long run that usually takes you 1 hour and 40 minutes to complete and you're scheduled for 5 x 1 minute surges with 5 minutes rest, you should begin the surges at mile 5, which will result in the last surge occurring at around mile 8.

The length of the surge itself, the rest in-between the interval and the starting point of the surge during the run are all variables that you can adjust to make the workout harder or easier. Typically, most runners start out with 4 x 1 minute surges with 5 minutes normal pace (normal being your average long run pace) between each. Runners at a very high level may progress to 6 x 2 minute surges with 3 to 4 minutes rest.

The pace of the surge should be anywhere from 5k pace to 8k pace. The exact pace will depend on the length of the surge and how much rest is given between hard efforts; typically, the longer the surge, the slower the pace.

Fast finish long runs

Long runs for the marathon are a staple of every training plan – no doubt about it. To prepare optimally for the marathon distance, it's critical that you train for the specific demands of the race. If you want to record a new marathon PR, this means teaching your body how to run faster on tired legs, depleted fuel and late into the race. To accomplish this, you can use a training concept called fast finish long runs.

What's the goal of a fast finish long run?

Mentally, the fast finish long runs simulate late-race fatigue and help train your body to push through the tiredness and pick up the pace, even when your legs are begging you to stop. When you get to that point in the marathon race, whether it be 18 miles or 22 miles, you'll have the confidence from your fast finish long runs to push hard and keep increasing the effort.

Physiologically, you're teaching your body how to burn fat more efficiently while running at marathon pace or faster. Late in the long run, and late in the race, you'll be low on carbohydrates and your body will be looking for alternative fuel sources. By simulating this situation in training, your body can adapt and more efficiently switch to burning fat as its fuel source.

How to run a fast finish long run

You should schedule a fast finish long run every second or third long run once you've established a good base mileage for your long run. That's usually 14 to 16 miles, but this number is different for every runner and is dependent upon your overall training plan.

An 18-mile fast finish long run might look something like this on your training schedule: 18 mile long run w/miles 13-16 at "x:xx" pace or faster. In this case, x:xx represents a pace that is between 10 to 15 seconds faster than goal marathon pace. For example, a 4-hour marathoner might look for a pace of around 8:55-9:00 minutes per mile as a starting pace.

So, the execution of the workout would look like:

- Run miles 1-13 at your normal easy run pace. Don't push too hard, too early – this is a tough run.

- Starting at mile 13, bring your pace down to the time on your training schedule. In this example, you would be running miles 13, 14, 15 and 16 at the up-tempo pace. After the first 2 miles at this pace, you can start to creep your pace faster than the defined pace if you're feeling good. Once you have 1 mile or less to go, you can start pushing the pace as hard as you can.

- The final two miles, miles 17 and 18 in this example, are run at your normal easy pace. It's sort of like a cool down, but you're still maintaining a good pace and you don't stop unless you absolutely need to.

Part of the training plan as a whole

Fast finish long runs, in combination with steady runs before the long run, help simulate late race fatigue while more specifically targeting the energy demands of the race compared with traditional long and slow runs. More importantly, fast finish long runs and surge long runs enable you to minimize injury risk while maximizing the benefits of each run.

Because fast finish long runs can be tiring and difficult, you shouldn't include them on your training schedule every week. Sometimes, you need to relax and just put time on your feet, especially while you build up your distance.

More than just the marathon

While discussion thus far has been focused specifically on the marathon, fast finish long runs have their place in 5k to half-marathon training as well.

The mental and physiological adaptations produced by the workout are much the same for shorter distances as they are for the marathon. With any race distance, the ultimate goal is to train the body to finish the competition as fast as possible. Even for 10k or half-marathon runners, running fast the last 1 or 2 miles of the race is a difficult task, thanks to tired legs and low energy stores. By simulating that experience in training, you'll be better prepared on race day to finish strong.

Strides for speed and running form

As just discussed with the long run surges, implementing short bouts of speed workouts into your marathon training plan will help you improve your mechanics and efficiency. Another way to develop speed in marathon training without sacrificing a workout day is with strides. Strides are 20- to 35-second sprints at your mile race pace, or roughly 85 to 95 percent effort. Typically, they are assigned to a running schedule after an easy recovery run or before a big workout or race. Strides are also used as part of the warm-up process to help get the blood flowing to your legs and your heart rate elevated.

How to do strides

You should stretch lightly before you start your series of strides, just to be sure everything is loose and ready to go. It is important to ease into the pace, and not explode out of the gate, when starting out. Explosive sprints are another training tool entirely.

When you've reached full speed, focus on staying relaxed and letting your body do the work. Keep a relaxed face, make sure your arms aren't flailing and work on landing on your midfoot (closer to your toes), not your heel. Continue to **stay relaxed** at your top speed and gradually, over the last 5 to 10 seconds, slow yourself to a stop.

Take a **full recovery** between each stride, which could be between 2 or 3 minutes, and repeat for as many times as your schedule dictates. You don't want to be breathing hard when you start the next one.

What are the benefits?

Strides have many benefits and can be used in a multitude of fashions depending on what each runner is trying to accomplish.

1. Strides help you **work on your mechanics** in short increments. It's easy to focus on form when you're only running for 20 to 30 seconds and you're not overly tired. Not only does it help you create mental cues to **stay on your toes and feel relaxed**, but it makes the process more natural for the body during the race.
2. As distance runners, we spend most of our time running at slower speeds to build our aerobic systems or work on our threshold. Strides offer you a great way to **inject some speed work into your training** plan without having to sacrifice a whole day of training. Just a few strides a couple of days a week will inject some "get-down speed" into your legs.

3. Strides are a great **precursor to faster, more rigorous training**. For many beginner runners, before they start doing any workouts, they should do strides. Because they may not be used to going fast or doing speed work, strides are a gentle introduction for the body and help them get used to the feeling of running faster.

4. Finally, strides can serve as a great way to **stretch out the legs after an easy session.** Often, especially in marathon training, the legs can get stale with the mileage and tempo runs. Strides help break up the monotony and add a little spice to the training and your legs. A few stride sessions are usually enough to get your marathon-weary legs feeling fresh again.

Cutdown runs

To improve your running, you need to train to the specific demands of the race. While each race distance has its own specific physiological demands, they all share one common element: As the race progresses, it becomes harder and harder to maintain goal race pace.

To exemplify this statement, let's look at a typical 10k race. Assume your goal is to run 45 minutes for your next 10k, which averages out to around a 7:15 per mile pace. Assuming you've trained correctly, the first mile at 7:15 pace should feel relatively comfortable. Actually, in adrenaline-pumping, competitive race conditions, it will feel downright easy (which is the reason so many runners start out too fast and is another topic altogether). As you ease into the race, a 7:15 pace for mile 2 will still feel relatively comfortable. At mile 3, you'll start to notice that your breathing is getting heavier and your legs are growing increasingly tired. By mile 4, the comfortable 7:15 pace at mile 1 is now becoming a pretty tough pace to handle. Your arms are heavy, your legs don't seem to be giving you as much power as they used to, and your breathing resembles that of a 75-year-old emphysema patient. Your pace begins to slip as you approach mile 5 and soon your dreams of a new personal best are out the window.

Well, that description of a 10k race sounded a little bleak. However, the point of the story is that, during a race, you need to constantly increase your effort just to maintain your goal pace. While mile 1 will feel calm and easy, by the last third of the race, goal pace will feel like an all-out effort. So, if you want to give yourself every opportunity to succeed on race day, you need to practice for this physiologic demand during your training. You need to train to increase your effort over time; you need to train to be prepared for this increase in fatigue; finally, despite what RunnersWorld might tell you, you need to train to push through the pain (which sounds scary, but it's really not all that bad).

To simulate these conditions, use what are called cutdown runs. The idea is to start the workout at 20 to 30 seconds slower than marathon pace and drop 10 seconds per mile until you are running just a bit faster than half-marathon pace. By doing so, you're teaching your body how to continually increase its effort as the workout continues and you become increasingly fatigued. That way, when you approach the midpoint in a race – when you start to feel the effect of the early miles – you instinctively learn to increase your effort and push harder to maintain your pace.

Furthermore, many runners are familiar with tempo runs and threshold runs that are designed to have you running just below or at your threshold pace (the point at which you can no longer get rid of the lactic acid produced by your muscles). By running just under your lactate threshold you can begin to decrease (or improve, depending on how you look at it) the pace at which you begin to produce too much lactic acid. These workouts are a great way to train for one physiologic piece of the race. However, during a race we never stop at our anaerobic threshold – we push through that threshold to keep running faster. Cutdown runs teach you to approach that threshold and then push through that point and test yourself. Combined with tempo runs during a training cycle, cutdown runs allow you to blend specific components of training into an overall strategy that addresses all aspects of the race.

An example

An example cutdown workout for someone attempting to break 2 hours in the half-marathon would look something like this:

1 mile warm-up, 6 mile cutdown run (9:45, 9:35, 9:25, 9:15, 9:05, 8:55), 1 mile cool down.

Modifying cutdown runs

Just like any workout, sometimes it's important to mix things up in the training to ensure that the body is always experiencing a new stimulus and therefore always adapting and never getting stale. Sometimes, instead of controlling the pace over the last 1 or 2 miles of a cutdown run, athletes should run the last mile "as fast as they can." This can add a fun challenge to the workout and really teach your body how to dig deep. This "fast as you can" last mile also helps develops confidence in closing speed and ability. Most cutdown runs are 5 to 8 miles in distance, but you can make them longer – say, 8 to 10 miles – by slowing down the early miles. These longer cutdowns can be a great medium-effort workout for marathon runners.

This is one of the most frequent questions about cutdown runs. Progression runs have been a hot training concept over the last few years, especially in the context of a long run. The main difference between a progression run and a cutdown run is the structure. A cutdown run requires you to run at a specific pace, which is also teaching your body how to pace itself – another skill that is vital to race-day success. Progression runs tend to be more free-form and a little longer. A progression run might start at easy pace for a few miles and then ask you to slowly creep your pace up and finish at marathon pace or maybe a little faster by the end, but without a specific pace drop-down for each mile. It's a little more of a "run as you feel" type of workout. These progression runs are great during long runs when you want to do something other than run long and slow, but aren't a specific workout like cutdown runs.

By developing the skill during your training to increase your effort and push harder as you get tired, you approach race day with the tools necessary to address the specific demands of the race. Too often, runners enter races with no specific training for what they will encounter during the race.

Alternating tempos

Improving your lactate threshold is one of the most efficient ways to train yourself to run faster at any distance over 10k. Luckily for runners, there is more than one way to improve your lactate threshold, so you don't have to keep doing the same workouts over and over. Mixing up workouts can keep you mentally fresh and motivated over a long training segment. One favorite variation on lactate threshold workouts is the alternating tempo.

What is an alternating tempo?

As you learned in the section on aerobic vs. anaerobic training, our bodies can only "clear" or reconvert a certain amount of lactic acid back into energy before the lactate floods our system and causes fatigue. To race faster, we must teach our body to clear lactate more efficiently.

Simple tempo runs and threshold intervals help your body develop this skill by gradually increasing the level of lactate in your system and allowing your body to slowly adapt to the increased lactic acid levels. However, if you can flood the body with lactic acid by running at a fast pace and then drop back to half-marathon or marathon pace to "recover," the body will respond by becoming more efficient at clearing lactate while running fast.

Simply speaking, you're trying to adapt the body to clear lactate more efficiently while still running at race pace. For the marathon and half-marathon racing, this means that you can more effectively use lactate as a fuel source and run faster or farther with less corresponding fatigue.

Alternating tempos are not races

When performing alternating tempos, running as hard as you can or faster than the prescribed "recovery" pace isn't better. You won't be allowing your body to become more efficient at clearing lactate. This is why it's important for runners to understand the workouts they are performing. By understanding the structure of the workout and its intended benefits, you're better able to stay on target and maximize the benefits.

Alternating tempos teach your body how to adapt to race situations

While we would all love to execute the perfect race plan each time out, it rarely happens. Sometimes in a race, you need to surge to get around other runners or you accidentally get sucked into a pace that is too fast by the runner next to you. The increase in pace spikes your production of lactic acid, and now your body needs to process the excess lactate as quickly as possible. If all you do in training is perform basic tempo runs, you're less likely to adapt to this increase in lactate and you will start to slow down.

One rule for better racing is that you should never expect your body to perform something on race day that you haven't done in training. This idea applies directly to why you want to include alternating tempos in your training and why they are part of our training plans at RunnersConnect.

How alternating tempos work

Alternating tempos are a more advanced training technique, so make sure you have done a few tempo runs already and you're ready to handle the change in stimulus. For marathon and half-marathon training, try alternating between 10 seconds faster than marathon pace and 5 to 10 seconds slower than 10k pace.

For a 3:30 marathon runner, the workout would look like this:

1-3 mile warm-up, 6 miles at (7:50, 7:25, 7:50, 7:25, 7:50, 7:25 – no rest), 1-2 mile cool down.

As you get fitter, you can increase the distance of the run to 7-10 miles depending on your normal workout volume. The total workout, not including the warm-up and cool down, is 6 miles. This workout is also a good chance to hone your pacing skills. You don't need to start sprinting to achieve the faster pace on the schedule; let yourself adapt over a 10 to 20 second period and adjust to the correct pace.

Tempo intervals

Tempo intervals are simply tempo runs that are broken into bite-size intervals to help you run longer at your threshold pace, or have an opportunity to run faster than you would for a normal tempo run. On your training schedule, they may look something like this:

1-3 mile w/u, 2 x 3 miles @ target pace w/3-5 minutes rest, 1-2 mile c/d

1-3 mile w/u, 3 x 2 miles @ target pace w/2-4 minutes rest, 1-2 mile c/d

1-3 mile w/u, 3 miles, 2 miles, 3 miles @ target pace w/2-5 minutes rest, 1-2 mile c/d

The exact combination of interval distances will change throughout your training plan as you introduce new stimuli, manage fatigue or target specific energy systems.

The rest in these examples are given as a range because the exact rest periods between intervals are based on your ability level, current fitness and goals. Likewise, the pace is based on your fitness level and will fluctuate at different points in the training cycle. Typically, your target pace will be between 12k and 10 seconds slower than half-marathon pace.

Purpose

As mentioned earlier, the main benefit to tempo intervals is the opportunity to either run longer at threshold pace or to run faster than threshold pace while still maintaining a high overall volume. To explain a little more in-depth:

Your lactate threshold is defined as the fastest pace you can run without generating more lactic acid than your body can utilize and reconvert back into energy. This pace usually corresponds to 10-mile or half-marathon race pace. Most runners can hold their lactate threshold pace for 20 to 40 minutes in training, depending on how fit they are and the exact pace they are running.

So, by breaking up the tempo run into two or three segments that are 20 to 30 minutes in duration, you can run 50 to 80 minutes at your threshold pace. This enables you to spend twice as much time during one training session improving your lactate threshold compared with a normal tempo run. Likewise, you can also run these 20 to 30 minutes tempo intervals at a faster pace than you might have been able to hold for a tempo run lasting 40 to 50 minutes all at once. Here is a graph to help you visualize this concept:

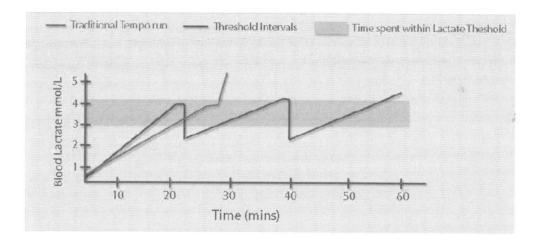

Tempo intervals are also advantageous because the rest between hard intervals gives you a mental break and can help you more easily tackle the workout. Instead of worrying about having to finish 6 miles all at once, you can focus on each interval one at a time and go far beyond what you believed you could do on the day.

Performing tempo intervals is pretty straight forward. Your training schedule will assign you a specific pace to target for the entire workout and your main goal should be to stay within that target pace range as best you can. For example, you may have a workout that looks like this:

2 mile w/u, 2 x 3 miles @ 7:00 – 7:10 pace w/4 min rest, 2 mile c/d

1. To perform this workout, you would run an easy 2 mile warm-up, which includes light stretching and a few strides to loosen up, to begin.
2. You will then begin you first 3 mile segment with a target goal of 7:10 for the first mile. If you hit 7:10 and feel comfortable, you can speed up to 7:00 or 7:05. If 7:10 felt difficult, remain at 7:10 pace. Always start your workouts on the slower end of the suggested pace range and only increase the pace to the faster end of the range if you feel good.
3. After you have finished running the first 3 mile segment you will rest for 4 minutes, which can be either walking or slow jogging, before beginning the last 3 mile interval.
4. Run the second 3 mile repeat as you did the first and finish the run with an easy 2 mile cool down.

Coaches' notes

- Concentrate on one interval at a time. Some of the tempo interval workouts can seem daunting, but if you just focus on completing each segment to the best of your ability and not worry about what is to come ahead, you'll get through the workout easier.

- Always start your workouts on the slower end of the suggested pace range and only increase the pace to the faster end of the range if you feel good.

- If you're struggling during the workout, don't be afraid to slow the target pace down to something you can handle. We all have our off days, whether due to outside stress or just a bad running day. Don't beat yourself up and simply focus on getting in as much of the workout as you can.

How to recover from hard workouts

Running fast workouts and nailing long runs is a key part of the training process. However, one of the most often-neglected aspects of training, especially since runners are almost always obsessed with pushing harder each day, is the recovery process. This section is going to outline "the optimal recovery process."

Not everyone will have the time necessary to perform this routine after every hard workout. Some might be able to fit it in after long runs, others might be able to see it through once per month. While this is the ideal recovery plan, you're free to pick and choose what you're able to fit in after each workout. For example, the simplest elements, hydration and refueling, should be easy to get in after every run, while the ice bath is a nice treat when you have the time. On a side note, this is what separates professional runners from the rest of the pack: In addition to running, drills and strength training each day, elite runners will often spend 1 to 4 hours per day on recovery – it's possible when you have the time.

After a hard workout or a tough long run, you should begin by hydrating as much as you can within the first 10 to 15 minutes. Even if the temperature was cool, or downright cold, you still sweat a significant amount and you need to replace the fluid loss. An electrolyte solution like Gatorade works best and you should aim for 16 to 20 ounces of fluid. RunnersConnect has also experimented with glucose tablets (made for diabetics) directly after running, especially when traveling. The tablet is pure glucose, which stimulates the insulin response in the body and ignites the recovery process.

After you're hydrated, you can begin your stretching routine while also ingesting your post-run snack or beverage. This post-run fuel could be something like chocolate milk, Endurox, yogurt and granola, or a banana and peanut butter bagel with orange juice. You want to aim for a 4 to 1 ratio of carbohydrates to protein.

The stretching and post-run fueling should begin within 25 to 30 minutes of finishing your run. The stretching should last 10 to 15 minutes, focusing on the major muscle groups (quads, hamstrings, calves and hips) as well as anything that is nagging or felt sore on the run. If you have a foam roller and are experiencing any small injuries, roll out on the foam roller to alleviate any knots or tightness.

After stretching, it's time to hit the ice bath. Fill your bathtub with cold water and add ice until the temperature reaches a balmy 55 to 60 degrees Fahrenheit. If you don't have a thermometer, the ice should still completely melt, but it should take about 3 to 5 minutes for a normal-sized ice cube to do so. Next, grab a towel and your favorite magazine and submerse your entire lower body, up to your hips, in the water. The trick to ice baths is surviving the first 3 minutes. Bite the towel and dream about your biggest goals. This will help you get through the hardest part of the ordeal. After 3 minutes or so, you'll notice the temperature feels more temperate and you can actually relax a little. If you are a veteran ice bather, or just a masochistic human being, you can kick your legs a little to stir up the water. This will help circulate the warm water surrounding your body and make things cold again. Remain in the tub for 10 to 15 minutes. The more you ice bath, the more comfortable this process becomes. After letting all the water drain from the tub, go ahead and take your shower. Your legs will feel cold for a few hours, but your muscles will thank you later.

After the ice bath, you'll want to ensure that you get a well-balanced meal in your system. So far, you've had Gatorade and some light snacks. To completely refuel, your muscles need something more substantial. If you run in the morning, this could be breakfast – egg whites with veggies and whole wheat toast, oatmeal with fruit and toast, even think pancakes are a decent choice if you top with fruit and yogurt. Lunch or dinner could be salad with a sandwich, pasta or leftovers from the night before. You just want to consume a high-quality meal with a good balance of carbohydrates, proteins and fats. This will provide your body with the final nutrients it needs to top off the recovery process.

After your meal, put your feet up, take a nap and follow it up with a massage. This is where things can seem "ridiculous," as massages and naps are an extreme luxury; however, this is the "optimal" recovery guide, after all.

About 60 to 90 minutes before bed, you should take a warm/hot bath in Epsom salts. Combine 4 cups Epsom salts with 1 cup baking soda and relax in the hot water for 10 to 15 minutes. After the bath, dry off and roll out your muscles with The Stick and get in a good stretching session. Not only will this help remove excess toxins from the muscles, the stretching before bed will ensure that you wake up feeling ready to go for your next run. Furthermore, the relaxing bath and the Epsom salts will help you sleep.

To sum up this routine in one easy-to-visualize chart:

1. Hydrate as soon after your run as possible with Gatorade or electrolyte drink.

2. Stretch major muscle groups and anything that is sore or tight. Roll out any nagging injuries or problem areas.

3. Eat a small meal that contains a 4 to 1 ratio of carbohydrates to protein.

4. Take an ice bath.

5. Eat a decent-sized, healthy meal.

6. Nap, put your feet up or get a massage.

7. Take an Epsom salts bath.

8. Roll out on The Stick and stretch well.

9. Get plenty of sleep.

As you can see, this routine is quite extensive. You won't always have the time to get in all of these recovery protocols, but it does give you glimpse of the things you could do on those rare occasions. Do what you can, but at least now you have a plan.

Scheduling down weeks

Analogies help to explain complicated physiological processes to runners in a way that not only helps them understand the science behind what they're doing, but also makes it practical. So, the best way to explain why adding planned down weeks into your training schedule is important – without referring to physiological terms such as cytokine levels (ck), troponin levels, and cardiac output – is to use an analogy or metaphor.

Visualize the body like a sponge, and your training like the water coming from a faucet. When you start training from scratch, you are like a dry sponge; you're ready to absorb all the training (water) that you can handle. So, you open up the faucet and let the training flow into your body, and you soak it all up. However, just like when doing dishes, too much water too fast can saturate the sponge. Therefore, you need to turn on the faucet gently for best results (read: start slow and gradual with your training).

Over time, if you keep filling up the sponge (your body) with water (training), soon it won't be able to absorb any more, no matter how careful you are with the rate of water flow. Actually, you could turn the faucet on full blast and not much would happen. This is when you need a down week in your plan. Now, taking a week off from hard training is one of the hardest things for a runner to do, but it is definitely necessary at times – even if you hate doing the metaphorical dishes.

So, what does a down week do, exactly?

A down week is like squeezing the sponge into a bucket next to the sink. The bucket in this case represents the store of fitness you want to have available on race day to throw at your competition. After quickly wringing out the sponge (taking a down week), you can go back to training and you're once again able to absorb all the training you put in.

Now, all you have to do is repeat and take a down week from training whenever your body isn't responding (please note that it is important to always be changing your training stimulus, as well).

When should I take down weeks?

The better you get to know yourself as a runner, the more accurately you can predict when a down week is needed and should be scheduled. The exact frequency will be different for all runners and can be affected by things such as training history, age, sleep and your life outside running; furthermore, sometimes down weeks aren't planned. If you notice a decrease in performance or a greater than normal level of fatigue, adding an impromptu down week might help you get you back on track.

Going back to the sponge analogy, imagine you've now done the dishes every day with the same sponge for 2 months. Picture how beat-up, nasty and less absorbent that sponge would be. After training for a long time without a mental or physical break, your body might actually feel the same. So, you need to schedule some time off in-between training segments, especially between marathon training cycles (this is by far one of the biggest mistakes novice runners make – and elites, too, since they can often get greedy for the next big marathon payday). In addition, if you take a longer break between training cycles, your sponge will be bigger and more absorbent when you come back now that you've had a solid block of training behind you. This means you'll be able to absorb more training faster and squeeze more water out of your running.

What to do when a workout doesn't go well

Sometimes, running can be like beating your head against the wall. The body is a complex organism with hundreds of complicated physiological processes occurring every second. On days when running feels effortless, all these elements "click" and you cruise through the streets. Unfortunately, sometimes you're out for a hard workout or an easy run and your body just doesn't want to cooperate and you feel like, let's face it, crap. These days can be some of the most confusing and frustrating parts of the training process.

So, what do you do when a run goes bad?

You have quite a few options when your body doesn't want to cooperate with your training schedule. However, the two best options when you get to the middle of a workout and you realize you just don't have it are to: (1) slow the pace; or (2) stop the workout and put it behind you.

Adjusting the pace

It's best to slow the pace of the workout instead of lengthening the rest or shortening the interval.

The length of rest or an interval tend to be more specific to your goal race and training plan, whereas pace is typically more an estimation of the effort your coach thinks it should take to hit the specific physiological adaptation you're looking for. So, the first step should be to slow your pace to keep yourself in that effort range.

To clarify, when your training plan or coach assign you a certain pace for a workout, they are estimating how fast you need to run to elicit a certain effort based on your abilities, fatigue levels and progression in the training plan. When the body isn't operating on all cylinders, the assigned pace is no longer a correct estimation of the effort level needed to accomplish the workout. By slowing the pace, you give yourself a chance to run within the physiological parameters of the workout and still get some benefit.

On the other hand, the rest and the interval length are usually a factor of the race distance or the physiological system you're working on. For example, a workout like 6 x 1 mile at 10k pace with a short, 1 min rest is working on your lactate threshold. Lengthening the rest takes you out of that zone and you diminish the benefits of the workout.

Of course, some days you just don't have it and you'll need to stop completely, but if you can complete the workout at a slower pace, you can usually get most of the benefits from the run and still keep the progression moving forward.

Sometimes you're really having a bad day and everything feels off. If you feel sick to your stomach, you're getting headaches or you're running more than 30 seconds slower than your goal pace for the workout, stop the run and jog back slowly to the car or house.

It's definitely not an easy mental task for a runner to stop a workout, but sometimes it's actually the best way move forward and get faster. When you're struggling this much to complete a workout, it's better to recoup, put the workout behind you and just move forward with the training.

It's important that you do not try to make up the workout the next day.

This throws off the balance of the training program and could lead to injury or overtraining. This is the No. 1 training mistake new runners make. Instead, evaluate why you had a bad workout – was it the heat? Stressful day at work or with the family? Went too hard on your easy day? Look for an answer and try to correct that fault for the next workout and put the bad day behind you. This can be mentally difficult, but in the long term it will keep you more consistent.

If you're a RunnersConnect member, you can always log into our coach chat and ask one of our expert coaches how you should adjust your training schedule to account for a bad workout. Making these kinds of adjustments is what can help take your racing to the next level, so don't hesitate to ask. If you don't have a coach, lean on the side of caution and give your body a rest and skip the workout – you'll be stronger and healthier in the long run.

Bad runs happen to the best of runners and it's bound to happen once or twice in every runner's training cycle. However, if you adjust the pace on the rough days and stop the workout on the really bad runs, you can stay consistent and ensure that the off day is merely a blip on the training

schedule.

Part III

Marathon Nutrition

Preventing the "bonk"

Close your eyes and imagine your body is a car; Corvette, Beetle, semi-truck, it doesn't matter as long as it uses gas. Whichever car you've envisioned yourself to be, assume your gas tank is large enough to hold about two hours of fuel at cruising speed (Note: Two hours is actually about the amount of fuel your body can hold while running at marathon effort). Now, if you were to run a marathon, how many miles would you get before you ran out of fuel? Here's a hint – it's your pace in minutes per mile.

Let's say you plan on running the marathon at 6 minutes per mile. Given our example, you'll hit the 20-mile mark just as you begin to run out of fuel. The problem quickly becomes apparent – you've still got 6.2 miles to go. However, the solution seems simple, doesn't it? Stop for gas at 13 miles and you'll be good to go for the rest of the race, right? In a word, yes; but stopping for fuel isn't going to help you set a new personal best. Furthermore, your body doesn't always digest the carbohydrates you take in while running. As your body becomes increasingly stressed, it begins to shut down non-essential functions such as the digestive system. So, while you could be consuming enough energy gels to keep a small nation alive, they may not be getting processed by your body – it's kind of like putting leaded fuel into your automobile.

Moreover, the problem of fuel during the marathon is further complicated because, just like an actual car, the faster you drive, the faster you burn through your fuel. If you've ever sped along the highway and compared your miles per gallon at 55 mph and 80 mph you'll understand this concept. Burning fuel while running is very similar to what you would experience in a car. The faster you attempt to run, the faster you burn through your available fuel. Similarly, if you run slow enough, your body will use its available fat stores as an energy source instead of glycogen, which means you can chug along for quite a long time, but at a very slow pace.

Now you can easily see the conundrum we're in when trying to train for a race like the marathon. Run fast and you'll burn out of fuel quickly and "bonk" in the process. Attempt to refuel the tank when too stressed or without practicing and your body will reject energy. So, what is a runner to do?

Enough about driving

The two best ways to address the problem of fuel during a marathon are: (1) to practice taking in small amounts of fuel while running fast; and (2) to train your body to burn more fat and less glycogen at higher speeds. Fueling during the race will be covered later, as this section will focus primarily on how to train your body to burn a greater percentage of fat while running at marathon pace.

If you want to set a new personal best, it's not enough to run just long and slow miles. Sure, you'll get used to the fatigued feeling in your legs and you'll gain the mental confidence from cracking the 20-mile barrier. However, long and slow miles aren't the best way to make you faster, which is why slogging through multiple 20- or 22-milers is not the best idea for marathoners with a goal of slower than 3:30. It's too much time spent running slow and thus not teaching your body how to burn fat at marathon pace. Instead, you need to: (1) practice running fast while tired; and (2) teach your body to become more efficient at marathon pace.

Breaking up your long runs

One of the best ways to get in volume similar to that of a 20- or 22-miler, yet maintain a faster pace, is to break up your long run into two moderately fast long runs. For example, instead of running 22 miles on a Saturday, try running 10 miles Saturday at a steady pace and follow it up with a 16-miler Sunday, with the last few miles at or near marathon pace. You'll carry the fatigue of Saturday's run into Sunday, which will simulate the latter stages of the marathon. However, you won't be so fatigued that you can't run fast at the end of the 16-miler.

In this plan, you've now run 26 miles for the weekend, as opposed to 22, and you've completed a good 60 percent of the run at or near marathon pace, compared to almost none during the 20-miler. That's 60 percent more time teaching your body to burn fat at marathon pace as opposed to just slow and easy running. Furthermore, running 22 miles at once will require a significant increase in recovery time, resulting in four to five days of nothing but slow, easy running. By breaking your run into 10- and 16-mile efforts, you'll recover within two or three days, which means returning to more marathon-paced work sooner than you otherwise would have been able to.

Practice running fast

Many beginning runners wonder why they need to do speed work during marathon training. If the race doesn't require you to run faster than 8 minutes per mile, why would you need to run faster? Again, the more efficient your body becomes at burning fuel while running fast, the longer you can run marathon pace on race day. Workouts such as threshold intervals enable your body to maintain a marathon effort while running faster than marathon pace, while also learning to burn fat more efficiently.

In addition, training elements such as strides can help you work on your mechanics and form, which will make running faster feel easier. If running marathon pace becomes less of an effort, you'll burn less carbohydrates for each mile run (remember more effort means your body utilizes a greater percentage of carbohydrate).

Developing and practicing your nutrition strategy

Practice makes perfect. Any baseball, basketball or football player will tell you it's been a mantra repeated to them throughout their years of competitive play. Unfortunately, runners often forget this time-honored rule when it comes to racing. We get so preoccupied with the physiological training adaptations needed to make gains in fitness that we often forget that racing itself is a skill. This is especially true in the marathon because, on top of skills like pacing and mental toughness, you're adding the variable of consuming energy and fluids.

Getting your stomach accustomed to eating and drinking on the run

One of the main problems with eating and drinking on the run is that it is difficult for your body to process the nutrition you consume. As you run farther and harder, your body becomes increasingly distressed. As your effort continues to increase, your body diverts energy from non-essential functions, such as digestion, to your muscles and brain to keep you going at the pace you're running. So, when you consume those energy gels and jelly beans, it takes much longer for them to get processed into the blood stream where they can be used by the muscles for energy. Sometimes, if the digestive system isn't working well at all, your body will actually reject the fuel or fluid you put in, which is why many marathoners experience stomach issues.

To train your body to become more efficient at processing nutrition while running, you need to practice during your training runs. However, this doesn't mean practicing taking energy while running at an easy pace – it's not specific to what you're doing in the race. You need to practice eating and drinking when your body is under duress, like during a marathon-paced run, tempo run or even during fast portions of your long run. This will specifically train your body to become more efficient at processing nutrition while running hard, which is exactly what you want to accomplish on race day.

Get even more specific

The running industry is filled with nutritional products that are designed to help you fuel during a marathon. You have gels, jelly beans, shot blocks, bars and of course a myriad of drinks such as Powerade and Gatorade. Therefore, it is important you find out which type of product you like best. For some, the consistency of gels will make them gag, while others love the taste of gels and their stomachs can't handle anything more solid. Each person reacts differently, so it is essential that you start practicing early in your training with different products to find the one you like best. Waiting until race day is a surefire way to fail.

If you think finding the right type or brand of energy product is difficult, you'll be sad to hear that you also need to find the right flavor. There are countless flavors available for energy gels and nutrition products; however, each one can react with your stomach in a different way. Also, don't just blindly trust what you think you normally like. One very good marathoner loved chocolate; yet, when he tried a chocolate energy gel during a marathon-paced run, he nearly puked the whole thing up. For a professed chocolate lover, it was near blasphemy, but it was an important lesson he learned in training.

While most of the products and brands are roughly equal in terms of quality, avoid those that contain protein. Your body can't digest it easily when running and, while it's been proven to help with recovery, there is no convincing science that proves it helps with fueling.

If you're going to rely on what products are available on the course, you must practice using them before race day. Do some research on the official race website and find out what will be offered on the course. Go to the store and get the same exact flavors and brands available on race day. This seems like overkill, but the slightest change in routine can leave you in for a rough day of racing. For example, in the 2008 Olympics, race favorite and 2:04 marathoner Paul Tergat finished a disappointing 10th place due to cramps caused by drinking cold water supplied by the race. During practice, Tergat was drinking fluids that were room temperature. In the marathon, you can't overplan.

Develop a strategy

Finally, it's important that you develop a nutrition strategy in advance of race day. This will include exactly when you'll plan on taking fluids and nutrition and how you plan on taking them. Will you bring you own water bottles or will you use the water stations available on the course? Will you walk through the stations or will you attempt to run through them?

Running or walking through the station is an individual choice, but if you're attempting to run sub-3:30 for the marathon you should run through them. However, slowing your pace a bit to ensure you maximize consumption is fine. If you're planning on a finish slower than 4 hours, you will benefit more from walking through the station and getting in as much fluid or fuel as possible.

If you're using your own water bottles, make sure you've practiced with them beforehand. You don't want any unnecessary chafing from wearing a water pack you didn't try first. If you're going to use the aid stations available on the course and plan on running through the water stops, head to the store and pick up some paper cups. Take them to the track, fill them with water and set up a table to put them on, or if you have young kids who love helping, you can have them hold the cups for you. Practice running at a little faster than marathon pace, grabbing a cup and taking a drink. The first couple of times you run through your makeshift water stop, more water will end up on the ground or up your nose. Here is a hint: Grab the cup and pinch it at the top on one end. This will make one end more of a funnel and also prevent the water from splashing out as easily. Also remember that you don't need to get all the water down in 5 seconds; you can take your time and breathe.

The marathon is a long event with the potential for many things to go wrong. However, the more you can practice during your training, the greater your chances of success. By developing a comprehensive fueling strategy that includes practicing the specifics outlined in this chapter, you'll be on your way to a great run on race day.

Eating and drinking during the race

Developing and executing a strategy for ingesting fluids and energy during the marathon is a crucial step towards success on race day. You can't expect to just wing it and drink and eat when feel like it if you want to run your best. Developing a race fueling strategy takes practice and intelligent planning.

Start drinking fluids early. Don't wait until you are thirsty or you're getting hot because, at that point, dehydration or glycogen depletion may already be starting. Furthermore, the more distressed your body becomes, the more difficult it is for your digestive system to process all the fluids and energy you take in. By taking in fluids early in the race, when you're not yet fatigued or stressed, you give your digestive system optimal conditions to get the electrolytes and sugars where they need to be.

Begin by taking fluids at the very first aid station available. Usually the first station comes right around the 5k mark. Ingest an electrolyte drink with sugar so you can keep your fuel levels topped off. Unless you're taking a GU, water is better on you during hot days than in you – opt for the Gatorade instead.

You should aim to take in 8 to 12 oz. of fluid every 5k. If it is a hot day you'll need to take in a bit more. Remember, you don't have to gulp everything down; you can take your time and carry the cup with you. If you hear sloshing in your stomach, you don't have to drink for the next 30 minutes, since this usually signals that your stomach is full.

What about energy gels or other solid energy sources?

Wait until the first 45 minutes to an hour to begin ingesting solid/gel fuels. This will usually occur between 5k and 10k, depending on how fast you are running. Waiting 45 minutes to an hour gives your body time to get in a rhythm, get comfortable and efficiently process the simple sugars you're ingesting.

When ingesting a gel/gummy/bar, make sure you always take it with water, not Gatorade. Both Gatorade and GUs contain high amounts of simple sugars. Combining the two means you're ingesting too much simple sugar at the same time. Your digestive system can't process it all, which may lead to cramps and side stitches.

Following this same logic, you should aim to consume a gel every 45 minutes to an hour. If you consume them too frequently, your digestive system might react negatively toward the high amount of sugar.

Post-workout nutrition

Perhaps the most important and often overlooked aspect of training, both for the elite athlete and the occasional exerciser, involves the recovery process and the refueling of the body. Every time you exercise, your body breaks down muscle fibers and creates micro-tears in your muscles. Ideally, the body repairs these little tears and actually makes them stronger. This process is how you get fitter and stronger with exercise. However, in order for your body to complete this rebuilding process, it needs the proper nutrients, and lots of them.

Ideally, nutrient intake should begin as soon as possible after finishing exercise and continue for about an hour to 90 minutes. During this time, you should consume a 4 to 1 ratio of carbohydrates to protein. This means that for every 4 grams of carbs you consume, you also need 1 gram of protein.

This formula may seem like a complicated system to add to your already-hectic training schedule. However, with very little planning and a few ideas from RunnersConnect, you can make it very easy. One top recovery tool is a product called Endurox. However, because it can be a little pricey (look online for the best deal), you can consider a few other nutrition options.

If you are at the gym, a good suggestion is Gatorade and an energy bar. Both are portable and will stay good even in your gym bag. At home, you have a wider range of options. If you prefer liquids, you can go with chocolate milk – yes, chocolate milk. Or try yogurt with a bagel or some granola.

No matter what you choose as your recovery food of choice, make sure you consume it as soon after exercise as possible. The body has a small window of optimal nutrient absorption, and you want to make sure you utilize as much of that window as possible.

What to eat before a run

What should I eat before I run? It's an age-old question faced by many runners both new to the sport and who have been training seriously and are looking to fine-tune their training diet. While you won't find one specific super-food that works for every runner, by providing some simple guidelines on nutritional requirements and timing, this section will help you find the perfect food for your pre-run snacks or meals.

Step 1: Timing your pre-run meals

The most critical variable in the equation is timing – how long before your run you can, or should, eat. Like most aspects of training, finding the optimal time to eat before a run is an individual preference. Some people can run within 15 to 20 minutes of eating almost anything short of a full meal and have no stomach issues whatsoever. Conversely, others can't muster a step out the door if they have eaten anything within 2 hours of the run. You need to find work works for you.

Conduct an experiment

To find your optimal timing window, try eating a medium-sized snack 90 minutes before your next run (see the last portion of this section for what constitutes a medium-sized snack). If your stomach handles it well, try moving the same snack closer to the run by 15 to 20 minutes. Likewise, if you experience stomach issues, push back the timing of your snack 15 to 20 minutes further away from the run. Keep moving forward or backward 15 to 20 minutes per run until you find the closest time you can eat before you start experiencing stomach or cramping issues.

Now you have a concrete number for how close to your run you can eat, which is the first step in determining your optimal pre-run meal or snack. In general, the harder you have to run, the further back your snack should be from this time threshold. Likewise, the larger the meal or snack, the further you'll have to push back from your closest pre-run eating time.

Step 2: Determine the nutritional demands of your run

Most runners severely overestimate the number of calories they burn and the amount of carbohydrates they need to complete runs under 90 minutes. The body has enough glycogen stored in the muscles from your normal diet to run at marathon pace for right around 2 hours. This means you don't need to load up on carbohydrates or calories before most of your normal training sessions, but might want a little extra fuel for harder workouts or long runs.

Demands of a normal easy training run

A 155-pound runner will burn between 600 and 700 calories on a 60 minute run, depending on his or her pace and effort level. To see how many calories you burn while running, you can try our running calorie calculator. Since you already have enough fuel in your muscles to run for 2 hours, and you might only burn 600 to 700 calories, you don't need a huge snack or meal before you head out the door.

For normal easy run days, a small snack 30 to 90 minutes before your run is all you need to stave off hunger and provide a small boost to your blood sugar levels.

Long runs and harder workouts

If you have a long run or workout that is going to take more than 90 minutes to complete, you should try and get a little something in your stomach to give you some extra fuel. A medium-sized snack or small meal 30 to 120 minutes before your run is optimal. The amount of time you need to eat before your run is dependent upon your timing experiment from Step 1.

Morning runners

If you are an early morning runner, you might have a little less glycogen stored in your muscles since you're coming off 6 to 8 hours of not eating, but unless you have a long run or a really hard workout, you don't need to worry too much about eating something before running. If you do have a longer run scheduled, try a small snack about 30 minutes before you head out the door. Otherwise, you don't have to worry too much.

Step 3. Find a food that sits well in your stomach

The most important aspect of a pre-run meal is finding something that agrees with your digestive system. While bananas may be perfect for your running friend, if they give you heartburn, avoid them. As with timing, you may need to experiment on your easy training runs to see what works best for you. This way, on important workout days and race day, you'll know exactly what foods sit well with you.

Basically, you're looking for easily digestible foods. Avoid fatty or high-fiber foods, which sit in your stomach and take longer to digest. Ideally, you want a snack with a good blend of simple and complex carbohydrates and maybe a dab of protein to help you feel fuller.

Need some pre-run snack ideas? Try these.

Small snacks

Energy bars – These tend to be light on the stomach and easy to digest. Avoid diet products, as these often cut the carbs, and those are exactly what you're looking for.

Natural energy bars – A granola bar is a great way to eat more naturally, but still stick with a light snack filled with carbs.

Bananas – High in carbs and potassium.

Small bowl of oatmeal – While oatmeal tends to have a good amount of fiber, it can still be a good solution for runners who can't eat close to run time, but need something small to sustain them.

Medium snacks

Toast with peanut butter and jelly – There is a reason your mom always gave you toast when you had an upset stomach. It's easy to digest and light on the stomach.

Wheat bagel with peanut butter or cream cheese – A little more substantial than the toast, with a small dab of protein to stave off hunger.

Yogurt and granola – A power pack of simple and complex carbs.

These are just some sample ideas of what you can eat before a run to stay energized and prevent stomach cramps. While eating before a run is highly individualized, with a few simple experiments, you can find the optimal pre-run meal or snack for you. By fueling properly and not eating too little or too much before you head out for your long training runs, you can maximize your training and start seeing results sooner.

Long runs on an empty stomach or fully fueled

Running coaches and exercise physiologists have long debated the potential benefits and possible disadvantages to performing long runs during marathon training on an empty stomach or fully fueled. Unfortunately, scientific literature hasn't provided runners with a clear-cut answer to that question. However, by looking at the available evidence, and combining that with practical examples, you can see how to use both in your training to maximize performance.

The role of glycogen

One of the most important determinants of marathon success is how efficiently your body can use fat as a fuel source as opposed to carbohydrates. The more readily you can burn fat while running at marathon pace, the longer your glycogen stores will last – providing crucial energy for that last 10k.

Your body has a limited supply of glycogen available to fuel your working muscles. Most research has shown that you can run about 2 hours at marathon intensity before you run out of glycogen. For all but the fastest runners in the world, this is going to leave you far short of your goal.

Unfortunately, while helpful in extending glycogen stores, simply eating on the run won't entirely replace all the glycogen you burn. Midrace fueling is limited by how quickly your digestive system can deliver the glycogen to your bloodstream and, under the duress of marathon racing, the stomach is not very efficient.

Therefore, it is critical that you find ways to optimize the amount of fat you burn while running at marathon pace. One of the most obvious places to look for these improvements is in the long run.

The case for glycogen-depleted long runs

The theory behind running your long runs on low glycogen stores is that by not having readily available muscle glycogen to burn, you body is forced burn fat. Consequently, your body will become more efficient at using fat as a fuel source. The real question is, does this theory hold true?

A recent study conducted in New Zealand showed that cyclists who completed exercise early in the morning without eating breakfast (fasted state) improved muscle glycogen stores by as much as 50 percent over the riders who ate breakfast before their exercise. Similar studies have made it clear that *occasional* fasting before exercise can improve glycogen storage and endurance performance.

However, other studies have gone further and tested the effects of training with low glycogen levels for more than one run or for extended periods of time. The research concludes that **extended carbohydrate depletion impairs performance** and does not enhance fat utilization.

The research makes a strong case that occasional long runs in a fasted state will improve glycogen storage and fat utilization, but extended training or multiple long runs in the fasted state will impair performance and do not provide further benefits to fat utilization.

The case for glycogen-loaded long runs

During a marathon training cycle, you have a finite number of workouts and long runs from which you can gain fitness. Therefore, it is important to maximize each opportunity to make progress. Completing long runs in a glycogen-loaded state increases the chance that you will be able to complete the run to the best of your ability, improving the overall quality of your long run.

Furthermore, carbohydrate intake before a long run aids post-run recovery by reducing muscle fatigue and overall damage to the muscle fibers. Likewise, glycogen loading prior to the long run provides the muscles with essential nutrients that promote the restoration of glycogen for subsequent sessions, improving the consistency of your training.

Finally, practicing fluid and nutrient intake during your hard training sessions is essential for race day success. Not only do you need to practice the skill of drinking from a cup while running fast, but you need to train your stomach to handle liquids and gels without getting upset.

Practical applications

With scientific evidence supporting long runs in both the fasted and glycogen-loaded state, how do you decide which is best for your marathon performance? Methodically utilize both approaches in your training.

You should run your early training segment long runs in a glycogen-depleted state. This will teach your body to boost glycogen stores and increase fat as a fuel source early in the training cycle. However, because the long runs won't be too long, you don't run a high risk of bonking and sacrificing a critical 20- or 22-mile long run.

Run your last 3 quality long runs in a glycogen-loaded state. In doing so, you will increase the overall quality of these important long runs, enabling you to finish faster and recover more quickly. Likewise, you can practice your marathon nutrition strategy to acclimatize your stomach to processing simple sugars and fluids efficiently.

By implementing both glycogen-depleted and glycogen-loaded long runs, you can improve the critical fuel efficiency element of the marathon while maintaining consistency in your training.

How to use energy gels

It wasn't long ago that runners relied solely on water, sports drinks and maybe some flat cola as their primary carbohydrate supplements during marathons and half-marathons. Luckily, our understanding of sports nutrition (specifically how glycogen is used during the marathon) has improved to the point that we now have a plethora of products to choose from, each designed to speed glycogen to our working muscles.

The problem these days is not in finding a glycogen delivery product, but rather in sorting through the myriad of possible choices and then developing a nutrition strategy to ensure optimal fueling on race day.

So, this section will outline exactly how energy gels and other carbohydrate supplements work, which will help you understand exactly when and how often you should be taking them to ensure maximum performance and fueling on race day.

How energy gels work

Your body uses two primary sources of fuel to feed the muscles when you're running – fat and carbohydrates. Fat is a largely abundant resource, but is broken down into usable energy slowly, making it an ineffective fuel source when running anything faster than about 60 to 70 percent of your VO2max (roughly equivalent to your aerobic threshold or marathon pace).

Therefore, your body relies on carbohydrates as its primary fuel source when racing. Generally, the faster you run, the greater the percentage of fuel will come from carbohydrates. The problem with carbohydrates is that you can only store a limited amount in our muscles – even when you load up. Typically, you can store about 90 minutes of muscle glycogen when running at half-marathon pace and about 2 hours when running at marathon pace. So, if you're not an elite, you'll be running out of muscle glycogen long before you cross the finish line.

Simply speaking, energy gels are designed to replenish carbohydrate stores that are depleted when running. Sounds like energy gels are a savior, right? Unfortunately, energy gels don't provide a simple 1-to-1 replacement (something you won't read on the label of your favorite gel) because the glycogen you ingest from gels doesn't always make its way to the working muscles.

Why?

Because carbohydrates are stored in both the muscles and the blood, and your performance on race day relies on using the glycogen stored in the muscles. For glycogen to make its way to the muscles, it must first be digested, make its way through the intestinal wall and then be absorbed by the muscles. This process takes time and isn't very efficient.

However, gels will often "wake you up" in a very noticeable way because your brain only runs on the glucose stored in the blood. As the muscles start to absorb more blood glucose, the brain gets less glucose and starts to get hazy (you've probably noticed this feeling on your long runs or if you ran without eating enough). Often, a gel will wake you up and help the mind feel energized, but it doesn't necessarily prevent the bonk in your legs.

In summary, energy gels help replenish the glycogen and calories you're burning when racing hard. However, they aren't very efficient or a simple 1-to-1 replacement, so timing and frequency are critical factors to avoiding the bonk.

When you should take energy gels

Just like almost every facet of running, the timing of when you should take your gels is individual. Each runner absorbs and processes carbohydrates at a different rate – some can feel the effect within 3 minutes while others might take up to 15 minutes.

This variation in absorption rate has to do with how well your stomach reacts to the gel. When running hard, your body often diverts blood away from the digestive track to help your legs continue to move forward (your body naturally conserves resources). Sometimes, your body shuts the stomach down completely, while other times it just slows down. This is why it isn't uncommon to see runners throw up fluids or gels right after ingesting them late into the race.

Therefore, you want to begin taking gels relatively early into the race. By taking the gels early, your body shouldn't be under great duress and you have a better chance of processing the sugars faster and without stomach issues. Take your first gel somewhere between 45 to 60 minutes, depending on how well you generally react to gels in training.

Some runners like to take a gel right before the gun goes off. While there is no problem with this from a physiological standpoint, it is better to consume a more substantial breakfast, with less simple sugars. This helps you avoid eating nothing but simple sugars for 3 to 4 hours. As discussed earlier, you can try a bagel with peanut butter, an energy bar or oatmeal.

How often should you take energy gels?

As we've already discussed, the speed at which you're able to digest and process energy gels plays an important role in how often you want to take them. Because the digestion process will be slowed or halted the farther you get into the race, you need to be careful not to overload your stomach. Therefore, wait about 45 to 60 minutes between gels before taking another one. Most runners should be closer to the 60-minute mark, especially if they have sensitive stomachs.

The second reason to wait 45 to 60 minutes between taking gels is that you don't want to speed too much simple sugar into your blood stream at once. Remember, the simple sugars from the energy gels will first be absorbed into your blood stream as glucose. The sugar will stay in the blood stream until absorbed by the working muscles or other organs. If you continue to pump sugar into the blood stream, you'll suffer the same fate as your children if left alone on Halloween – getting sick from too much sugar.

The other aspect to keep in mind is that your digestive track is trainable like most every other part of your body. So if you eat gels in training, particularly if you do it at set intervals that correlate to when you will take them during the race, your body will learn to keep the digestive track running and you will digest the gel more readily. This is why it's critical you practice your exact fueling strategy as often as possible in training.

General tips about energy gels

Now that you've learned some of the basics of how energy gels work and how to properly strategize a marathon or half-marathon nutrition plan, here are some practical tips that can help you execute on race day.

How to take gels if you have problems

Like we've discussed, it's possible that your stomach might shut down during the latter half of the race. If this happens to you and you've been unable to take energy gels late in the race, try eating only a small portion of the gel, but in closer intervals. For example, eat 1/4 of the packet every 20 minutes. You'll still consume the energy you need, but you'll give your stomach a better chance to properly digest without getting sick.

Always take with water

Always take energy gels with water, never alone and never with Gatorade. Without water, energy gels will take longer to digest and enter the blood stream. If you take an energy gel with a sports drink, you run the risk of ingesting too much simple sugar at once. Taken together, a gel and sports drink could be delivering close to 60 grams of pure sugar – yuck.

Test out flavors and brands

Not all energy gels are the same. Some are more viscous, some taste better and each flavor can be delicious or wretched to another runner. The important thing is that you have to experiment and find something that works. At the 2008 Olympic Trials, Desi Davilla had trouble keeping down her fluids and gels. Everything she took in came back up. So, after fading to the finish, Desi implemented gels in practice, but even that process wasn't smooth. During long workouts, Desi would force herself to drink and eat gels, but her system still rejected it. In her own words: "It was actually kind of disgusting." However, knowing she could never make the podium if she didn't figure out the issue, Desi continued to force her body to adapt. Eventually, she found the right combination of gels and fluids to train her stomach to handle the sugars and she went on to run 2:22 in Boston. Next time you think "I just can't do it," imagine what an Olympian would say to that.

Why you might not lose weight when marathon training

While training for optimal performance on race day is the main focus for our coaches here at RunnersConnect, many of the athletes we coach set secondary goals to lose weight and generally desire to be healthier overall. Certainly, sometimes these two goals – setting a new PR and losing weight – go hand-in-hand, but as coaches we tend to focus on letting weight loss come naturally as the body adapts to training and new levels of fitness.

However, we can appreciate that runners might want to speed up the weight-loss aspect of training. Unfortunately, when a runner first begins serious training, sometimes the needle on the scale doesn't immediately go down, and sometimes it can even head in the wrong direction. This trend can be frustrating and demoralizing to many runners. However, if you understand the science behind initial weight loss and the practical reasons for why this occurs, you can temper yourself from getting discouraged and make positive and long-term gains both to your overall fitness and to your race times. So, here are some reasons why you might actually gain weight when training hard.

The scale is a trickster

If the scale were a human, he or she would be considered a trickster. A scale only provides one number, your absolute weight, which isn't always an accurate measurement of what is happening in your body. Drink a gallon of water and you've instantly gained 8.3 pounds. Remove a kidney and you've lost 2 pounds. Extreme examples, but they show that your absolute weight on a scale isn't always a truthful assessment of changes in your weight or, more importantly, your fitness. Here are just a few reasons the numbers on the scale will lie to you when you are training:

You will store extra water

When you increase your training to gear up for your goal race, your body begins to store more water to repair damaged muscle fibers and to deliver glycogen to the working muscles. Likewise, you may be drinking more water to supplement the miles and ensure you're hydrated. All this water can add pounds to the scale.

Muscle weighs more than fat

While you're not going to turn into a bodybuilder after just a few days of running, your body will slowly begin to build muscle and burn fat. While this is great news for your overall fitness and race times, you're actually gaining weight by replacing low-density fat tissue with high-density muscle tissue. While it may not look great on the scale, you may see a nice difference in the mirror. Replacing fat with muscle is much healthier and will help you continue to get faster and fitter.

It takes a deficit of 3,500 calories to lose 1 pound. Ideally, you should target a 300- to 600-calorie-a-day deficit if you want to lose weight safely and be healthy. This means you can expect to lose about 1 to 2 pounds per week. Checking the scale every morning is going to revel very little about your long-term progress or the actual state of your weight loss. If you weigh yourself every day, you're simply measuring day-to-day fluctuations in your hydration levels and other non-essential weight metrics. Just like you wouldn't expect a 1-minute drop in your 5k PR after a week of training, don't expect a 5-pound weight loss after your first week of running.

Eating too much to compensate

You burn more calories while running than almost any other activity you can do. Unfortunately, while the energy demands of running are high, this does not mean that you can eat a Big Mac and a doughnut guilt-free and still lose weight. Runners often rationalize their dessert intake by saying, "Hey, I ran 5 miles today, I deserve it." Likewise, many running groups meet up at Starbucks or the local coffee shop after a weekend run. Unfortunately, an iced latté and a small scone will quickly eliminate any caloric deficit from the run and negate possible weight loss. While running does burn calories, you have to be careful not to quickly or inadvertently eat them back with non-nutrient-dense foods.

Likewise, you should be providing your muscles with the necessary carbohydrates and protein to recover. This is a delicate balance, and probably the most difficult element to losing weight while running. It is more important to focus on recovery and ensure that your muscles have the nutrients they need to rebuild. The harder you train, the more often you will get hungry and the real secret is to refuel with nutrient-dense and high-quality foods. Sacrificing recovery for a few less calories is not a good long-term plan. The numbers on the scale are arbitrary and focusing on them can be detrimental to your long-term progression. If you can continue to build your fitness and training levels, you'll be running farther, faster and be much healthier overall.

Calculating how may calories you burn while running

On average, a runner will burn 100 calories per mile. You can determine how many calories you burn while running with RunnersConnect's running calorie calculator. This is a great resource and will help give you a better picture of how many calories you've burned so you can adequately refuel, but not overcompensate.

Hidden calories

Many marathon runners automatically assume they are going shed pounds with all the extra mileage they are putting in. However, not only should you ensure that you're recovering properly after your hard workouts and long runs by eating the right foods, you also need to account for "hidden calories." Primarily, hidden calories come in the form of sports drinks and energy gels, which have a high caloric content.

It's critical that you practice your fueling strategy during your long runs and hard workouts for optimal performance on race day. Likewise, to sustain high levels of training and to complete long and arduous marathon workouts, you need to fuel during your training sessions with sports drinks and energy gels.

However, this also means that the total number of calories you will burn from these long runs and hard workouts will be less than you might realize. Again, for optimal performance and training progression, you need these extra calories. Unfortunately, they can also be the reason you might not see the weight loss on a scale.

Focus on the right metrics

The bottom line is this: Running will not automatically result in an immediate weight loss. Yes, running burns more calories than any other form of exercise, but the scale should not be the primary metric by which you gauge your fitness level and training progression.

While I understand weight loss is an important goal for many runners, don't become a slave to the numbers on the scale. Pay attention to how you feel – do you have more energy, feel stronger, starting to fit into your clothes better? While not absolute measurements, these emotions are a much more accurate measurement of your progression.

Hydration

Most people have heard the saying "You must drink fluids" repeated over and over; well, duh, who doesn't drink when it's hot or they're running? However, this section will provide some background and science in laymen's terms explaining why you need to use sports drinks, when it is best to use them and what is the best type.

To begin, it is important to note that the critical factor in hydration is how rapidly fluids can be absorbed into the blood stream. The absorption of fluids into the body is largely dependent upon the composition of the fluids in terms of their carbohydrate (sugar), sodium (salt) and potassium concentrations. As a rule, the higher the carbohydrate content, the slower the absorption rate. Thus, your choice of sports beverage would depend on whether your primary aim was rehydration or the replenishment of energy (sugar or fuel) and electrolyte stores.

Before and during exercise, rehydration should be your main priority in order to maintain fluid balance, especially in the hot and humid summer months. Therefore, your best bet would be a sports drink diluted with water. Because of the high sugar content of most sports drinks, the fluid is not readily absorbed into the blood stream. By mixing half water and half sports drink, you provide your body with the best combination of electrolyte replacement and immediate absorption. Products are also available that contain pure electrolyte concentrations that you add to water. RunnersConnect's electrolyte replacement product of choice is Nuun.

However, after you are finished working out, water or a diluted sports drink isn't the best choice for your recovery needs. Water and diluted drinks do not contain enough of the sugars and electrolytes that your body needs in order to bring itself back into balance. In addition, because water or highly diluted drinks are so rapidly absorbed, consuming high quantities results in a rise in plasma volume (in non-technical terms, this means your body is now oversaturated with water). This rapid absorption leads to a further imbalance of electrolytes and frequent bathroom stops, which will only increase fluid loss and decrease your desire to drink.

Your best bet post-workout is a drink that contains a fair amount of sugars and electrolytes that will speed your recovery process and stay with you a little longer. In addition, after you feel hydrated and are finished sweating through your running clothes, you should start to begin your post-run recovery fueling.

Side stitches and cramps

While there have been a lot of articles written about what exactly a side stitch is and how to prevent one – not eating too close to a run, stretching and walking are some ways – what do you do when it is too late and you've already got one?

Most conventional wisdom says slow down, stretch and wait until the ache subsides. Great advice when you're not in the middle of a race, an important workout or running with a group! Luckily, some sage coach many years ago had a great suggestion; expand and contract your diaphragm in the opposite direction it naturally wants to. Confused? Let's explain.

Put your hand on your stomach and take a deep breath. Which way does your stomach move? It expands, correct. As in your stomach moves up against your hand. Now, keeping your hand on your stomach, breath out all the way; this time your stomach contracted or moved down, right?

When you have a cramp, force your stomach to do the opposite of what it naturally wants to do, which is expand when you breathe in and contract when you breathe out. It's a little difficult to get the hang of at first, but practice a few times and it will become easier. Once you've got the rhythm down pat, make your breaths deep and forceful, taking all the air in that you can, every little gulp you can manage – and letting it all out, forcing out every molecule. Do this a few times on the run and your cramp will disappear.

You'll still have to slow a little at first because of the change in breathing rhythm, but you won't have to stop completely. The more you do it, the better you'll get and the more efficient at relieving cramps you'll become.

Part IV

The marathon taper

How to taper

You've pushed through tired legs on your long runs; hit the track for speed workouts until your shoes were soaked with sweat; and recorded enough miles to put your car to shame. With three weeks to go until the big race, all the hard work is done, right? Well, yes and no. While all the physical work is in the bag, ensuring success on race day requires special attention to the marathon taper. The marathon taper is a delicate balance of maintaining fitness while promoting recovery.

Three weeks before goal race

1. Reduce weekly mileage to 85-90% of your maximum

It's actually not too difficult to reduce your mileage 15 percent. For example, if you're running 50 miles per week, you only need to cut out 7 miles from your weekly running routine. This can be done by giving yourself an extra rest day or by simply cutting out 2 or 3 miles from your regular recovery runs.

2. Maintain intensity

Some training plans begin to drastically cut workout volumes starting three weeks out from the race. This is a mistake to avoid if you've been training diligently for 16 to 20 weeks. Physiologically, your body takes 10 days to realize the benefits from a workout and completely recover. As an insurance policy, perform your last workout 13 days prior to the marathon; starting the taper too early robs you of another potentially great workout.

Make sure your workout is specific to the marathon – you don't need any VO2max workouts or speed sessions at this point. The workout should be similar to what you've been doing during the rest of your training plan (i.e.

no need to get nervous and think you need to blast the best workout of your life).

3. Reduce long run volume 10-20%

You don't need to completely eliminate the long run yet, but you do want to avoid making yourself too tired. If your longest run so far was 20 miles, run anywhere from 16 to 18 miles. However, listen to your body. If you feel sluggish and tired, have the confidence to cut the long run back.

Two weeks before goal race

1. Reduce weekly mileage to 70-75% of maximum

Reducing the mileage this week is actually easier than the previous week. Your long run will be shorter and your intense workouts, which should be your biggest volume days, will also be reduced. For example, a 50-mile week will be reduced to 35 to 38 miles. With no long run and less-intense workouts, your easy recovery miles should remain relatively stable or minus only a mile or two.

2. One medium-intensity workout

Your last workout of any real difficulty should be on Monday or Tuesday. The volume of this workout should be reduced to 60 to 70 percent of your normal hard day. For example, if your tempo intervals usually total 9 miles, this workout should be about 6 miles in total distance. Again, make sure the workout is marathon specific, so no VO2max workouts. This is a good opportunity for you to practice marathon pace.

3. Reduce long run 50-60%

At this point in your training, the "hay is in the barn." You can't gain any more fitness, but you can certainly tire yourself out. The distance of this run is more a psychological boost to keep you in a routine and to prevent you from feeling like you're doing nothing. If you're feeling fatigued, don't hesitate to back off the mileage and opt for a shorter distance.

The week of the race

1. Significantly reduce mileage

If you thought training was tough, wait until you try to reduce your mileage the week before a marathon. It takes discipline and confidence to give your body the rest it needs. You should consider giving yourself an extra rest day while reducing your daily runs to 50 to 60 percent of their normal volume. So, if you're used to running 8 miles on your easy recovery days, you should target 5 to 6 miles instead.

2. One mini fartlek session

Do one very easy fartlek session to help alleviate nerves and to remind your body what marathon pace feels like. Perform a workout like: 15-20 minute warm-up, 6-8 x 2 minutes at marathon pace with 2 minutes easy running between, 10-15 minute cool down. This workout won't leave you fatigued, but it will give you a little bit of confidence and nice pop in your step.

3. Run the day before the marathon

Run the day before the marathon. Try running anywhere from 1 to 3 miles very easy. Running will help promote blood flow your legs and will make you less nervous. Running the day before a race also stimulates the central nervous system, which will enable your legs to respond better the following morning.

The marathon taper is filled with anxiety and nerves. No matter your ability level, remember that you've put in the training and don't go overboard either direction on the taper.

Common tapering mistakes

Tapering might be one of the most feared words in a runner's vocabulary, right next to "patience" and "rest." After months of long miles and lung busting intervals, finding the right balance of sharpening and rest to hit race day firing on all cylinders can be a nerve-wracking process. Even more daunting is that the taper isn't an exact science. Ask any 10 coaches and researchers what the optimal taper would be and you'll get 10 different answers.

However, coaches and scientists do agree on a few principles that are constant in the perfect taper. Unfortunately, these universal elements are also the most frequent aspects runners botch in the last two weeks of their training. Here's how you can avoid the three most common tapering mistakes:

Mistake #1: Dropping mileage too much

As race day approaches, many runners significantly reduce their volume in the last 7 to 10 days before the competition. The conventional theory is that the legs need a rest from all the mileage to perform optimally. However, when we take a deeper look at what effect easy aerobic mileage has on the body, both from a recovery and fitness-building perspective, the fallacy of significantly dropping volume becomes apparent.

By design, easy running is supposed to help you recover. An easy run increases blood flow to the muscles specific to running, helping to clear out waste products and deliver fresh oxygen and nutrients. If your recovery runs during the hardest portion of your training cycle have enabled you to adequately recover between hard workouts, what would change the 10 days before your race, when you're not performing intense workouts? Nothing changes. Significantly reducing your mileage does not result in faster recovery or more rested legs if your current volume has allowed you to recover properly during training.

Furthermore, when you look the specific demands of long-distance running, you clearly see a heavy reliance on aerobic respiration as a primary energy system:

Event	Male		Female	
	% aerobic	% anaerobic	% aerobic	% anaerobic
5k	88	12	90	10
2 mile	84	16	88	12
1 mile	76	23	86	14
800m	60	39	70	30
400m	43	57	45	55

Duffield, R., Dawson, B., & Goodman, C. (2005). Energy system contribution to 1500- and 3000-metre track running. *Journal of Sports Sciences*, 23(10), 993-1002

Since the aerobic contribution to events longer than 2 miles is greater than 85 percent, significantly reducing the specific component of training that provides the most value to aerobic conditioning is flawed. To perform your best, you need to continue to train your aerobic system without producing fatigue.

What you can do

Instead of dropping your total training volume in the last 7 to 10 days before your race, keep your easy aerobic running at the same mileage as you are adapted to in training. Then, reduce your volume 20 percent the third day, 30 percent the second day and 50 percent the final day before the race. This will eliminate any possible fatigue, yet still allow you to maximize aerobic gains.

Mistake #2: Getting off your normal routine

The body craves consistency. The more routine a runner can be in his or her training, whether it be the time of day he or she runs or the number of days per week he or she trains, the better the body will respond. Many runners can experience the difference between being on a routine and being inconsistent just by fluctuating the time of day they run. Something as simple as changing your morning run to an afternoon run can make a huge difference in how optimally the body is prepared to perform.

Unfortunately, in an effort to reduce volume or find a magical way to feel more rested, runners with often stray from their normal routine during the taper. Consequently, their legs feel flat or they have less-than-optimal training runs, reducing confidence heading into the big day.

What you can do

Stay on your routine as best you can. If you normally run five days per week, exercise five days per week. If you double (run twice per day), make sure you have a few double runs thrown in. Do whatever you can to trick your body into thinking the taper is like any other training week.

If you're nervous about keeping the frequency of training so high, you can turn to other forms of light exercise. When training for big races, go for an afternoon walk when you don't have a double run scheduled. If your body is conditioned to running twice per day, this can be a great way to keep yourself on a consistent routine and calm the nerves.

Mistake #3: Thinking the race is going to feel good

Many runners think the taper is going to be some magical process that will make them feel unstoppable on race day. The misleading notion is that the legs will feel so rested and the body so prepared that something special and unbelievable is going to happen on the race course. Sorry, folks, not going to happen. Running a PR hurts! No matter how well rested or prepared the body is, racing hurts. If runners toe the starting line thinking that somehow they're going to feel anything different, they're in for a rude awakening halfway through the race. Consequently, when the race gets tough, these athletes question their ability and their training, as opposed to accepting the challenge and realizing pushing through the pain is a part of racing.

What you can do

Prepare yourself mentally. Don't head into the race telling yourself that somehow this race is going to be different. Be prepared for it to hurt, but remember that you've trained yourself to push through this exact situation. Visualize the race during your training runs or while meditating and picture yourself hitting that point in the race when your body starts to hurt. Recall those feelings from your last race or hard workout and then visualize yourself pushing through that moment. By preparing yourself mentally, you'll be ready to face the realities of the race.

Implement these three tips and avoid the most common mistakes when tapering for your next race and you'll be more consistent with your results.

Visualization to improve chances of success

As runners, we're always looking for that extra edge in training to make us faster and more consistent on the race course. Understandably, most of our efforts to improve are geared towards the physical – lowering lactate threshold, increasing muscle power, improving form. Enhancement to any of these physiological systems is going to result in faster race times and should be the main focus of your training plan. However, if you're already pushing your physical training boundaries, it's possible that adding mental planning and visualization to your regimen can help you squeeze out that extra 1 or 2 percent on race day.

Some of the world's top athletes, from professional golfers to Olympic track and field medalists, practice mental imagery and visualization in their training. Perhaps one of the most well-known examples of the power of mental imagery is the gold-medal performance of Mark Plaatjes at the World Championships marathon in 1993. Plaatjes extensively practiced visualization techniques while preparing for the World Championships, so much so that he knew every undulation on the course and had "run" every possible scenario of the race before he arrived in Germany. When the real racing began, Plaatjes was able to summon his reservoir of confidence and mental preparation over the final miles and snatch victory just 3 minutes from the finishing line.

Mental training and visualization clearly works for high-caliber athletes. Here are some specific visualization and mental planning tips and strategies you can implement to improve your performance:

You can practice visualization techniques in your training to prepare for every possible scenario and improve your execution on race day. All it takes is 10 to 15 minutes a day to increase your chances of success.

Be specific and detailed

When visualizing your race, be as specific and detailed as possible. Imagine yourself at the starting line, surrounded by thousands of other high-strung runners – is it hot, is it cold, what are you wearing? When the gun sounds, envision the acceleration in your heart rate and the claustrophobic feeling as the stampede begins. By conjuring up these emotions, sights and sounds, you can prepare yourself to remain calm and collected, and execute your race plan in a chaotic environment. The more specific you can be with the sights, sounds and emotions, the more calm and confident you'll be on race day.

Visualize the good and the bad

Likewise, visualize positive and negative scenarios. Let's face it, no matter how fit you are, a race is going to hurt at some point. Imagine yourself working through those bad moments during the race. This way, when they inevitably occur, you'll know exactly what to do and be confident you can work through them.

Furthermore, visualize what you'll do and how you will feel should something go wrong. What if your shoe comes untied or you have to go the bathroom? By visualizing these scenarios, you'll have a specific plan in place and instead of panicking, you'll be calm, cool, and collected.

Boost your confidence

Another advantage of visualization in training is the opportunity to boost your confidence. It's been well documented that high confidence correlates to an increased level of performance. By visualizing yourself succeeding, you can subconsciously improve your belief in yourself and your abilities.

To enhance your self-confidence, try implementing self-affirmation and self-talk into your daily routine. Spend 5 minutes each night before bed standing in front of the mirror repeating specific, positive messages to yourself. The mirror helps engage the visual receptors in the brain and helps internalize the positive messages. Phrases such as "I am fit, I am fast, I am going to win" tend to work well. Create your own self-affirmation phrase and spend 5 minutes repeating it to yourself. Before you know it, there won't be a doubt in your mind you're going to perform on race day.

Before the race

As race time approaches, you can't help but get nervous. After all the hard work you've put in, you don't want it to go to waste. Luckily, you can implement the visualization techniques you used in training to reduce these pre race nerves.

Recollect all your great workouts

If you find yourself getting nervous before the race, start thinking back to all the great workouts you had during your training. Think back to that great tempo run you had where you floated effortlessly over the road, or visualize your last successful race and begin to conjure up those same feelings of accomplishment.

Focus on what you can control

We get nervous when we don't know the outcome of things, like when the killer is going to jump out of the shower in a scary movie or how we're going to feel halfway through the race. Take the focus off those elements of the race you can't control (your finishing time, your opponents, the weather) and direct them to outcomes you can control. Visualize yourself executing your race plan, going through your warm-up routine and even focusing on your breathing. By directing your thoughts to those physical and mental aspects you can control, the nerves will dissipate and you'll increase your chances of success.

During the race

Racing is tough, there's no two ways about it. At some point on your way to a great race or a new PR, you're going to hurt and you're going to have self-doubts. Letting negative thoughts creep into your mind is one of the easiest ways to derail your performance.

Stay positive with self-affirmation and self-talk

Before you begin the race, decide on a few easy-to-remember mantras that will help you gain confidence and persevere through any rough patches during a race. Make sure all the words in your mantra are positive. For example, use "I am strong; I can do this," as opposed to "Push through the pain; don't give up." The second mantra elicits negative connotations with the words "pain" and "give up."

Likewise, you can employ mental cues to remind yourself to focus on proper form when going up a hill or when you start to get tired. The mantra "Relax and go" in the last mile of a race could remind you not to tighten your face and shoulders as you get tired. Find your positive mantra and use it when the going gets tough.

Granted, no amount of mental imagery and visualization during training and racing will compensate for a poor training regimen. However, if you're already pushing your physical limits and want to take your race performances to another level, incorporating visualization techniques into your training and racing can provide the advantage you need.

The last few days before the race

As marathons continually increase in size and more and more runners choose to run destination marathons, the planning and logistics the last week before a marathon are becoming increasingly important. To reduce pre-race nerves and help ensure nothing goes awry in the week before the marathon, here are some great tips and important guidelines:

Flight and travel

Pack your race gear in your carry-on baggage if you're flying to the race. Put any casual clothes on checked baggage if you are going to check luggage. Casual clothes and shoes are great to have, but your whole trip depends on you having your running gear. Plus, if your checked bag gets lost, you're going to be surrounded by runners all weekend anyway, so being stuck in running clothes for a day or two won't make you look weird at all.

When you're packing, lay all your gear out on the bed so you can see it all and do a quick check at a glance. Don't forget Band-Aids, chafing prevention and nutritional products (usually energy gels and electrolytes) that you plan to use in the race. Pack these in the carry-on bag. Leave nothing to chance.

Carry food with you at all times. In the peaking phase, you never want to get hungry (especially the last 3 days before the race). Don't overeat, but be prepared in case a meeting at work goes long, you hit traffic on the drive to the race or you are late for a meal. Always have a good snack available.

In addition to your race gear, pack some good food in your carry-on bag. You may want something to eat on the plane/train/car. If you've flown in the last decade, you know how frustrating airlines can be with the arrival and departure times.

Try to keep fluids with you at all times as well. If you're flying, empty a water bottle before going through security so you can avoid buying the $4 bottle of water later. Don't over-drink, but be prepared.

Getting settled and your pre-race meal

The first thing you should do after settling into your hotel is find a grocery store. Ask the front desk for the nearest one or call ahead to expedite the process. Go immediately to the grocery store and stock up. Buy the foods you like and you know prepare you best for a good race, such as bagels, peanut butter and jelly, energy bars, yogurt and sandwiches. If you've practiced your marathon nutrition properly, you already know what works for you. Don't just eat out of nervousness, but have food available if you need a snack.

Plan ahead for your meal on the night before the race. There are likely many runners and families coming to the race. Restaurants fill up before both big and small-town marathons. Getting a pasta dinner on a normal Saturday night in Chicago or New York can be tough, but finding an open table when 50,000 runners are trying to do the same thing is next to impossible. If you're racing in a small city, the marathon is the only show in town, so things will get booked quickly. Call ahead and find a place you'd like to eat and make reservations. Don't leave your meal to chance. Find a relaxing place and enjoy a nice comforting dinner.

Try to eat close to your hotel so you can take a leisurely 10 to 15 minute walk after dinner to help fend off nerves and give your stomach a chance to digest. Don't eat too early or too late, or you may be hungry or stuffed on race morning. As discussed in the marathon nutrition section, the last meal doesn't have to be huge. It's the meal two nights before that is most important.

The race expo and sightseeing

You'll likely need to visit the expo to pick up your race number, chip, etc. Enjoy the expo but don't spend all day there. It's too much time on your feet. Browse through it, pick up what you need and get out. The expo is where many runners get dehydrated and hungry, so carry fluids and fuel with you to keep this from happening.

Don't try anything new. Race expos are filled with companies selling or giving away products – clothing, food, gadgets. Don't eat anything you're not absolutely sure sits well with your stomach and don't be tempted to try a new clothing article if you haven't used it before. Enjoy the information, take in the camaraderie and save your new foods, gadgets and clothing for after the race.

If you're doing a destination marathon, plan your travel so sightseeing happens after the race. Walking around before the race will get your legs tired and defeat the whole purpose of your visit and all your hard training. Plus, sightseeing after the race is more relaxing (you're not stressed about the race) and it gives you a good chance to stretch out your legs.

The last week before the race can be stressful enough when you're nervous about performing your best. Add the marathon taper, travel and logistics to your already-frayed nerves and your PR can go up in smoke before you even hit the starting line. By methodically planning beforehand and following the tips in this section, you can eliminate potential issues and focus all your energy on running your best.

5-day pre-race nutrition plan

Marathon Rule #1: Never try anything new on race day

This ebook has already covered why you have to practice and plan every detail of your marathon race in training. In addition to clothing, pacing and training, this rule also applies to your nutrition strategy in the five days leading up to the race. You should not experiment with any new foods or venture too far from your normal diet. It's easy to get nervous in the last few days of your taper and be persuaded by a new product a friend recommends or you see at the race expo. However, if you haven't tried it before, especially at marathon pace or during a long run, don't be tempted.

It's also important that you experiment with the types, quantity and timing of the food you eat before you run. Some runners have very weak stomachs and need up to three hours to digest food before they can run comfortably. Other runners can eat within an hour of a hard run with no adverse side effects. It is important to figure out which type of runner you are and to take this information into account when you plan for the race morning.

Experiment with your pre-race meal before race day. Your last two long runs or difficult marathon-paced workouts should be similar to race simulations. Try wearing the clothes you think you'll wear on race day, the shoes, socks and everything you can think of. Eat the same pre-race meal you're planning for the night before the race and, when you wake up in the morning, eat the same breakfast you plan on having. This will give you time to change things up before race day if you find it doesn't work for you.

5 days from the race

Begin to increase your total carbohydrate intake by adding in more pastas and starches (low glycemic index foods) to your diet throughout the week. The old idea of depleting your carbohydrate stores the week before the race and binging on carbohydrates the last few days in an attempt to trick your body into overcompensating and storing more fuel is outdated. Ensuring that you consume a higher percentage of your total daily calories as carbohydrates is sufficient.

Remember, you're not running as much as you have been, so eating too much more than you normally do will make you feel bloated and lethargic. At this point in the nutrition cycle, relax and don't go overboard.

48 hours before the race

Your last big meal should be two nights before the race. It will give your body ample time to digest anything you eat so you won't feel bloated on the morning of the race. Too many people gorge on pasta the night before the race, only to reach the starting line the next day stuffed and lethargic. Have you ever tried to run the morning after Thanksgiving? If you have, you know the feeling and if you haven't, well, don't schedule a tough workout.

24 hours and before

Eat normal, balanced meals like you would do on any training day. Make sure you drink plenty of liquids all day long, especially electrolyte fluids such as Gatorade, or use electrolyte tabs such as Nuun. It helps if you carry a water bottle along with you throughout the day to remind yourself to drink.

Your main meals should still be in the form of low glycemic index foods. Ideally, you won't be too active on the day before the race, so you may feel full quickly. That is fine; you shouldn't try to stuff yourself.

18 hours before race

Start eating small meals every 2 to 3 hours, but after lunch, cut out red meat, fried foods, dairy products, fats, nuts and roughage. You should only be consuming light, digestible foods like energy bars, bread and small sandwiches. Keep drinking water and electrolyte beverages and avoid salty foods.

4 hours and less

You should be up early enough before the race to eat a small breakfast with plenty of time to start digestion before the gun goes off. You'll want to drink mostly water (unless you know temperatures at the race are going to be warm), with some electrolyte fluid. Don't try to get all your fluids down by chugging your water bottle. Drink small, regular-sized amounts. Room-temperature water is absorbed quicker than warm or cold water. You'll need approximately 6 oz. every hour or 8 oz. every hour on hot days.

Preparing for the elements

Running a marathon or half-marathon in the rain, cold or heat isn't an exciting thought. However, you can't change the weather, so the best strategy is to be prepared. This is a brief list of some innovative strategies and tips that you can implement on race day in the face of challenging weather:

Rain

If it's raining, take a trash bag, cut a hole for your head and wear it while you wait at the starting line. DO NOT RUN with the trash bag on for any distance; use it to keep yourself dry at the start. More than likely, you'll be standing in the starting corral for a long period of time before the race, with little shelter.

If you have friends/family on the course, give them a dry shirt or socks that you can swap at 16 or 20 miles to get a nice fresh feeling and to get rid of any soggy clothing or shoes that are holding you back.

If it's a very cold rain, using Vaseline on exposed body portions will help keep you warm. Vaseline is waterproof, which will help keep your hands and lower legs from getting too cold. One caution: Vaseline does not allow your body to sweat efficiently, so don't put in on your head and neck. You want excess heat (yes, there will be some even in such cold temperatures) to dissipate as needed.

Cold

If it's cold, find that ratty sweatshirt/pair of gloves/hat/sweatpants your spouse has been nagging you to throw out for years. If you don't have any clothing items ready to be ditched, head to Wal-Mart or a cheap clothing store and buy some warm-weather clothes you could run in for a mile or two. You can wear these warm items in the corral when you're standing in the cold and have nowhere to move to stay warm. Once you get running past the first mile or two, your body will begin to warm up and you can shed them. Most marathons pick up discarded clothing and donate it to charity.

Likewise, layers are key while actually running. Remember, you're bound to heat up as the race progresses, so having layers that are easy to remove will allow you to stay cool.

Heat

Heat is one of the most difficult elements to run a marathon in, so it's important that you prepare as best you can. Drink more fluids and electrolytes leading up to race morning. If you have a chance, make a slushy (freeze some Gatorade the night before the race) and bring it with you to the start. Recent researchers have proved that drinking something cold, like a slushy, 10 minutes before a race helped keep core body temperatures cooler and enabled runners to compete for 20 percent longer than with just a cool beverage.

Furthermore, adjust your race pace the first few miles to ensure you have enough energy to finish strong. You can see how heat will affect your running time and pace with the RunnersConnect temperature calculator.

Running a marathon is difficult under any conditions. By preparing ahead of time and implementing an innovative strategy, you can avoid any factors that will affect your race.

The optimal marathon race plan

If you've followed this guide, then you've practiced your nutrition strategy, you've completed the long runs, you've put together the perfect taper and you're ready for success on race day. The last missing piece is the marathon pacing and race strategy.

Putting "time in the bank" is bad!

If the recent financial crisis has showed us anything, it's that banks are evil. Just kidding! But in all seriousness, the theory of "putting time in the bank" during the first 13 miles of a marathon race is critically flawed. The bank will take your money and leave you crashing the last 10k just as it did the stock market.

It's not clear where the "time in the bank" theory came from, but the strategy has led to the demise of more marathon runners than any other source. The proper race strategy that will give you the best chance to PR actually follows the exact opposite theory. For a successful marathon race, you should target a pace that is 10 to 15 seconds per mile slower than your goal marathon pace for the first 3 or 4 miles.

Don't believe me? Here's an interesting statistic: Every world record, from 1,500 meters to the marathon, has been set running negative splits – running the first half of the race slightly slower than the second half. It's true; look it up if you have the time. This means that if you want to ensure that you run the fastest time possible, you have to be conservative during the early miles of the race. With the adrenaline and competition, this can be difficult and will require focus. You should practice this skill during your training runs. You can do this by entering tune-up races to simulate the adrenaline and fast pacing of early in the race. You can also accomplish this on training runs with strict adherence to pace, learning how these efforts feel and by using tempo runs.

Getting around other runners at the start

In addition to running the first 3 or 4 miles a bit slower than marathon pace, it is important that you stay relaxed while running in the big crowds and passing runners that you need to go around. Surging past slower runners and getting uncomfortable in the tight crowds is an easy way to ruin your race. All the surges and stopping and starting requires a lot of energy. Energy = fuel, so the more energy and fuel you burn up during the first few miles, the less you'll have over the last 10k. Try your best to set yourself in the right corral, and when the race starts, relax and go with the flow until a natural opening for running appears. As you've learned already, you should be planning on being a little slow for the first few miles anyway, so take a deep breath and focus on relaxing.

Pacing after the first 4 miles

After the first 3 or 4 miles, slowly creep your pace toward your goal marathon pace. It's still OK to be a little slow in these miles, as your conserved energy will allow you to hold pace the last 10k and avoid the dreaded marathon fade and bonk. During this time, you should concentrate on eating and drinking whenever possible and as much as you know your stomach can handle. Unlike time, you definitely want to put energy in the bank.

Why does running slower in the first half work?

Running a little slower than goal marathon pace for the first 3 or 4 miles works for two reasons: (1) by running slower, you conserve critical fuel and energy you'll need the last 10k; and (2) running slower gives your body a better chance to absorb and take on fuel and fluids.

Just like a car, the faster you run, the more fuel you burn. Almost everyone has seen the effects of fuel consumption while driving at 80 mph vs. 55 mph. Your body reacts in a similar way. When you run over your marathon pace (scientifically defined as your aerobic threshold), you start to burn significantly more carbohydrates. Similarly, weaving in and out of other runners the first few miles, which tends to happen more with runners who go out too fast, is like driving your car in the city. We all know cars get significantly reduced miles per gallon while driving in the city. Your body is the same way.

Your body can store enough fuel to run about 2 hours at marathon pace. This means unless you're running really fast, you'll need to take on a lot of extra carbohydrates during you run. As discussed previously, your body has a difficult time digesting the carbohydrates you take in while running. The best way to combat this unfortunate bodily function (besides practicing taking gels and fluids in practice) is to take on carbohydrates in fluids early in the race when your body is feeling good and not stressed. If you started the race a little slower, you'll have a chance to absorb more of the nutrition you take on board.

What about the last half of the race?

There is no way to sugar-coat racing: The last half of a marathon is tough. Sorry, folks, there is no way around it. From a race strategy perspective, if you've done the training, were conservative over the first few miles and have taken adequate fluids and carbohydrates, you're going run well the last 10k. However, to help along the way, implement some simple mental tricks.

Keep your mind and body relaxed. Look within yourself and focus on you. Think confident thoughts and repeat confident mantras to yourself: "I am fast; this feels good," or "I am strong; I'm running great." Every time you feel tired or feel the pace slip, repeat to yourself that you need to refocus and concentrate and get back on pace.

Oftentimes, you can watch a video of fast marathon runners and, when you start to hurt, you can imagine myself running like them. Good form – head straight, arms swinging forward and back slightly, powerful strides. Just having the mental imagery of good form can help you maintain your pace when the muscles become increasingly tired with each step.

If the pace starts to slip, throw in a surge to get your legs fired up again. Sometimes all it takes is a small burst of speed to reinvigorate your legs and pace. If you've done surges during your long run, this will be just like practice for you.

Finally, try to break the remaining distance into bite-size and easily digestible pieces. After doing lots of hard training runs, break the race up into one of your best previous workout sessions. For example, if you had a great 2 x 3 mile session, remember how it felt and think, "Hey, I did this workout before; let's get back on pace and do it again." Likewise, sometimes a mile can seem like a long distance, so break it down into a time instead. Thinking you only have 3 to 4 minutes until you hit the halfway point of a mile makes it seem a lot easier – 4 minutes is nothing!

Have fun!

This is the typical pre-race comment, but it's true. Running and racing are about having fun and enjoying yourself, so remember that when you start getting nervous about the race. If you've done the training and followed all of RunnersConnect's advice, you're going to run well. Enjoy the challenge and the atmosphere!

Part V

Sample Training Plan

Sample intermediate training plan

This sample training plan will help you visualize and put to action all the concepts this guide discusses. This plan was designed for an intermediate-level runner who can approach 50 miles per week in their training. If you're running more or less than 50 mpw, you can always adjust the easy day mileage to your average training distance.

Week	Day	Workout
Week # 16	Monday	Off or cross train
	Tuesday	5 miles easy
	Wednesday	Off
	Thursday	5 miles easy w/ 2 x 20 sec strides
	Friday	Off
	Saturday	4 miles easy w/3 x 20 sec strides
	Sunday	8 miles Long run
	Total	22 mpw
Week # 15	Monday	Off or cross train
	Tuesday	5 miles easy w/4 x 20 sec strides
	Wednesday	Off or cross train
	Thursday	1 mile warm-up, 4 miles @ Marathon Pace (MP), 1 mile cool down
	Friday	Off or cross train
	Saturday	5 miles easy
	Sunday	10 mile long run – all easy pace
	Total	26 mpw
Week # 14	Monday	Off or cross train
	Tuesday	6 miles easy w/ 5 x 20 sec strides
	Wednesday	4 miles easy
	Thursday	1 mile w/u, 6 miles @ MP, 1 mile c/d
	Friday	Off or cross train
	Saturday	5 miles easy
	Sunday	11 mile long run – all easy pace
	Total	34 mpw
Week # 13	Monday	Off or cross train
	Tuesday	7 miles easy w/ 5 x 20 sec strides
	Wednesday	4 miles easy

	Thursday	2 w/u, 2 x 3 miles @ half marathon pace (HMP) w/3min rest, 1 c/d
	Friday	Off
	Saturday	1 mile easy, 4 miles steady pace, 1 mile easy
	Sunday	12 mile long run – all easy pace
	Total	38 mpw
Week #12	Monday	Off or cross train
	Tuesday	7 miles easy w/ 5 x 20 sec strides
	Wednesday	4 miles easy
	Thursday	2 mile w/u, 4 x 1.5 miles @ 10 sec faster the HMP w/2min rest, 1 mile c/d
	Friday	Off or cross train
	Saturday	5 miles easy
	Sunday	13 mile long run w/ miles 9-12 @ Goal MP or faster
	Total	38 mpw
Week #11	Monday	Off or cross train
	Tuesday	5 miles easy with 4 x 30 sec strides
	Wednesday	Off or cross train
	Thursday	2 mile w/u, 6 miles @ MP, 1 mile c/d
	Friday	Off or cross train
	Saturday	5 miles easy w/5 x 20 sec strides
	Sunday	8 mile "long" run
	Total	27 mpw
Week #10	Monday	Off or cross train
	Tuesday	**2 w/u, 10 x 800 @ 12k pace w/1min rest, 1 c/d**
	Wednesday	5 miles easy
	Thursday	2 w/u, 6 miles @ HMP, 1 c/d
	Friday	Off or cross train
	Saturday	1 mile easy, 5 miles steady pace, 1 mile easy
	Sunday	14 mile long run w/4 x 60 sec surges @ 5k pace w/5min easy btwn starting at mile 5
	Total	43 mpw
Week #9	Monday	Off or cross train
	Tuesday	**2 w/u, 16 x 400 @ 8k - 10k pace w/45 sec rest, 1 c/d**
	Wednesday	5 miles easy
	Thursday	2 w/u, 3 x 2 miles @ 10 sec faster than Half Marathon Pace (HMP) w/3min rest, 1 c/d
	Friday	Off or cross train
	Saturday	1 mile easy, 5 miles steady pace, 1 mile easy
	Sunday	16 mile long run w/6 x 60 sec surges @ 5k pace w/5min easy btwn starting at mile 6
	Total	44 mpw
Week # 8	Monday	Off or cross train
	Tuesday	**2 w/u, 6 x 1-mile @ 10k-12k pace w/90 sec, 1 c/d**
	Wednesday	6 miles easy
	Thursday	2 w/u, 7 mile tempo run @ 15sec faster than MP, 1 c/d

	Friday	Off or cross train
	Saturday	1 mile easy, 5 miles steady pace, 1 mile easy
	Sunday	18 mile long run w/miles 12-15 @ MP or faster
	Total	50 mpw

	Monday	Off or cross train
	Tuesday	5 miles easy w/6 x 20 sec strides
	Wednesday	Off or cross train
Week # 7	Thursday	2 mile w/u, 6 miles @ MP, 1 mile c/d
	Friday	Off or cross train
	Saturday	6 miles easy w/6 x 20 sec strides
	Sunday	10 mile long run
	Total	30 mpw

	Monday	Off or cross train
	Tuesday	**2 w/u, 8 x 1000 w/30sec rest @ 10k pace, 1 c/d**
	Wednesday	6 miles easy
Week # 6	Thursday	2 w/u, 3 mile - 2 mile - 3 mile @ HMP w/3min rest, 1 c/d
	Friday	Off or cross train
	Saturday	1 mile easy, 5 miles steady pace, 1 mile easy
	Sunday	Long run 18 miles w/12-15 @ Goal MP
	Total	50 mpw

	Monday	Off or cross train
	Tuesday	**2 w/u, 6 x 1-mile @ 10k-12k pace w/90 sec, 1 c/d**
	Wednesday	6 miles easy
Week # 5	Thursday	2 w/u, 8 mile tempo run @ 10 sec faster than MP, 1 c/d
	Friday	Off or cross train
	Saturday	7 miles easy
	Sunday	14 mile long run w/6 x 90 sec surges @ 5k pace w/5min easy btwn starting at mile 6
	Total	47 mpw

	Monday	Off or cross train
	Tuesday	**2 w/u, 2 x 5 miles at 15 sec faster than MP w/4 min rest, 1 c/d**
	Wednesday	6 miles easy
Week # 4	Thursday	5 miles easy w/6 x 20 sec strides
	Friday	Off or cross train
	Saturday	1 mile easy, 6 miles steady pace, 1 mile easy
	Sunday	20 mile long run w/ miles 13-16 @ Goal MP
	Total	52 mpw

	Monday	Off
	Tuesday	6 miles easy – no strides
Week # 3	Wednesday	2 w/u, 7 mile tempo @ Goal MP, 1 c/d
	Thursday	Off

	Friday	**2 w/u, 8 x 800 @ 10k pace w/1min rest, 1 c/d**
	Saturday	5 miles easy
	Sunday	13 mile long run w/7 x 90 sec surges @ 5k pace w/5min easy btwn starting at mile 5
	Total	41 mpw
Week # 2	Monday	Off
	Tuesday	7 miles easy w/5 x 30 sec strides
	Wednesday	6 miles easy
	Thursday	1 w/u, 2 x 2.5 miles @ Goal MP w/3min rest, 1 c/d
	Friday	Off
	Saturday	5 miles easy
	Sunday	6 miles easy
	Total	31 mpw
Week # 1	Monday	Off
	Tuesday	3 mile w/u, 8 x 3 mins @ Goal MP w/2min easy btwn, 2 mile c/d
	Wednesday	4 miles easy
	Thursday	Off
	Friday	15 mins easy running
	Saturday	Race
	Sunday	Celebrate

Notes on the Sample Training Plan

Week 16: Introductory week

This week is a basic training week that eases you into the training program. All runs should be completed at a comfortable pace that is 60 to 90 seconds slower per mile than your goal marathon pace. If you do not have a goal marathon pace yet, this should be a pace that allows you to be conversational. If you enjoy swimming, cycling or weight training you can use the off days to include these activities.

Week 15: Introductory week #2

This week is a transition into some paced runs that will help make goal marathon pace feel more comfortable and allow you run the last 6 miles of he marathon and not just suffer through them. Tuesday – the strides will help improve your form and make you more efficient. Thursday – an easy workout that will just help get you used to running at marathon pace and help you determine where your fitness is at.

Week 14: Aerobic strength week

This is the first week that will help you build-up aerobic strength. Tuesday – more strides to improve form. They also serve as a good precursor to the speed work you will do later in training. Thursday – this is a marathon pace workout that will help get you accustomed to goal marathon pace and introduce your body to doing workouts.

Week 13: Aerobic strength week

Remember to vary up the locations of your runs and run on hilly routes to practice for the course. Run on soft surfaces such as dirt whenever you can in order to reduce the impact on your legs. Thursday – a continuation with the aerobic strength building by increasing the distance of your run, but breaking it up so you can run faster. The long run has continued to increase – don't slack on the distance since you'll be building the volume quickly.

Week 12: Aerobic strength week

At this point, you should be starting to feel more comfortable running marathon pace, although you will be getting tired from the increase in training. Thursday – breaking up the tempo run allows you to run at a faster pace and cover more distance without a drastic increase in effort. The 2 min rest should be an easy walk in order to help you get your heart rate back down. If possible, run on a measured course or with a Garmin to ensure that you are running on pace. Sunday – running marathon pace at the end of the long run will help simulate the fatigue at the end of the actual race.

Week 11: Recovery week

This is a built-in week of recovery to help you adapt to the increased training, ensure you remain injury free and help keep you motivated. The workouts are very easy and just enough to keep your legs feeling fresh without making you tired. The break will leave you feeling fresh and excited to attack the next three weeks.

Week 10: Anaerobic threshold week

The introduction of threshold intervals, which will help lower your anaerobic threshold and inject some speed into the training. Tuesday – preferably, these should be run on a track. Be sure not to start out too fast. Thursday – a continued progression of your threshold by increasing the distance to 6 miles at half-marathon pace, which will make marathon pace feel more comfortable.

Week 9: Anaerobic threshold week

Tuesday – 400 meter repeats to help improve your speed and mechanics while maintaining your threshold. It is better to start off a little slower and pick up the pace throughout the workout as you feel more comfortable. Thursday – breaking up the tempo run allows you to increase both the distance and the pace without drastically increasing the effort.

Week 8 - Anaerobic Threshold Week

One more anaerobic threshold-specific build-up week. Tuesday – mile repeats are a tough workout that will really have you working hard and will increase your level of fitness dramatically. Thursday – increasing the tempo run distance to 7 miles. The real training is starting to take shape. Remember, you'll have good runs and bad runs, especially on the long runs and workouts. We train to gain fitness for race day, not to prove how fit you are.

Week 7: Recovery week

Another built-in recovery week to allow you to absorb the previous three weeks of training and stay injury free. The light workouts this week are just to get the legs moving a little faster. The next three weeks are pretty tough and you'll need this week to get geared up for the last three tough weeks.

Week 6: Marathon-specific week

The workouts in the marathon-specific segment are geared towards the training elements most essential to the marathon. Tuesday – the 1,000 meter repeats are tough because you only have 30sec rest, which is very short. This will help drastically increase your threshold. DO NOT start too fast. Thursday – again, breaking up the tempo run into mentally manageable pieces. You should be able to run faster and cover the 8 miles.

Week 5: Marathon-specific week

Tuesday – the workout is the same premise as last week, but the interval distance increases, which will make the workout more difficult. Thursday – an 8-mile tempo will be one of the hardest workouts you'll do in training.

This would be a good run to practice your pre-race meal and to experiment with clothing options you might consider on race day.

Week 4: Marathon-specific week

Only two workouts this week: Tuesday – 2 x 5 miles is another marathon simulation that will not only increase your fitness but will be another great marathon practice run. An extra few days' rest and you have the longest run, 20 miles. The accumulative fatigue of the miles the day before plus the workouts will simulate the race as much as possible.

Week 3: Transition taper week

This will be the start of the taper. Since the marathon is 99 percent aerobic, make sure you don't eliminate that portion of the training. Therefore, the aerobic training, mileage and tempo runs will still be present in the training. Eliminating the final 10 percent of the hard workouts will help get your legs freshened up.

Week 2: Taper week

A continued lowering of the mileage and only one easy workout to help keep your body accustomed to marathon pace. Keep the runs easy and remember that nervousness is normal.

Week 1: Race week

Made in the USA
Middletown, DE
09 November 2017